Vouchers For School Choice
Challenge or Opportunity?

An American Jewish Reappraisal

Edited by
Marshall J. Breger and David M. Gordis

The Susan & David Wilstein Institute of Jewish Policy Studies

The Interdisciplinary Program in Law and Religion, Columbus School of Law, The Catholic University of America

Copyright © 1998 Wilstein Institute of Jewish Policy Studies

All rights reserved. No part of this publication may be reproduced, translated, or transmitted in any form or by any means without permission in writing from the Wilstein Institute of Jewish Policy Studies.

ISBN 1-893380-00-9

Printed in the United States of America

The efforts of Professor Marshall J. Breger,
co-convener of the conference
from which this volume has emanated,
have been inspired by the life and values of
his mother, Beatrice Breger,
who passed away during the preparation
of this manuscript. His colleagues in this
endeavor join him in dedicating this volume
to her memory.

Contents

Preface .... Zachary I. Heller		vii
Acknowledgements		ix

Introductions

School Vouchers: A Sympathetic View .... Marshall J. Breger		1
School Vouchers: A Skeptical View .... David M. Gordis		9

Section One: Implications of School Vouchers for Public Schools and for American Society

Introduction .... Jay Greene		15
School Choice in the History .... Jeffrey Henig of Education in the United States		19
The Milwaukee Experiment .... The Editors		25
The Cleveland Experiment .... Martin Plax		29
School Choice: What Does the .... Jay Greene Evidence Say?		37
Roman Catholic Perspectives ...... The Most Rev. James McHugh		43
A Minority Perspective .... Floyd Flake		47
The Effect Upon Public Schools: .... Chester Finn, Jr. Financing and Support		53

Section Two: School Voucher Programs and Traditional Principles of Church-State Separation

Introduction .... Marshall J. Breger		61
The History of "The Wall of Separation": .... Robert Destro Church and State in Constitutional Tradition		63
Remarks from a Roundtable .... Marc Stern Ronald Rotunda Sanford Levinson		79
Agostini and the Politics of the .... Robert Destro Establishment Clause		89
On "Doctrine" and the Establishment Clause ..... Michael Ariens		97
Reading the Tea Leaves: *Agostini* and Vouchers .... Steven Shapiro		105

The Plasticity of Power and the Supreme .... Marci Hamilton Court's Establishment Clause Jurisprudence	**109**
Agostini v. Felton: A 1997 Ruling .... Nathan Lewin for the Ages	**113**
Still a Limited Freedom: Religious Liberty .... Joseph Viteritti after *Agostini*	**117**
Equality, Not Preference or Discrimination .... Eugene M. Volokh	**121**

Section Three: Implications of a School Voucher Program for the Jewish Community

Introduction .... David M. Gordis	**129**
The Jewish Experience in American Public ..... Jonathan D. Sarna and Private Education	**131**
The Case of the Jewish Day School .... Alvin I. Schiff	**137**
The Financing of Jewish Day Schools .... Marvin Schick Jeremy Dauber	**145**
Dollars and Day Schools: the Baltimore .... Jay Bernstein Experience Larry Cohen	**157**
Jewish Day School Funding .... George Hanus	**165**
The School Voucher Dispute .... Elliott Abrams	**169**
The Jewish Community and School Choice ...... Jonathan Tobin	**175**
Rethinking Vouchers .... Avram Lyon	**179**
A Statement on Voucher Policy .... Jewish Council for Public Affairs (JCPA)	**183**
A Roundtable Discussion .... Melvin Shralow Barry Shrage David Zweibel Marvin Schick David Pollack Deborah Miller	**189**
Contributors	**201**

Preface

Zachary I. Heller

The question of school vouchers has been debated for decades both in the American Jewish community and within American society in general. The initial arguments revolved around church-state separation issues and the concern that vouchers would diminish support for the public school system, an American institution of great significance to most American Jews as the common gateway to acculturation. In recent years this issue has re-emerged high on the American-Jewish public policy agenda, both because of the critical condition of many inner-city public schools and because of the concern for expanded support for Jewish day schools as vehicles for strengthening Jewish identity through education. This renewed interest must also be viewed against the background of polarized political philosophies that often energize much of the debate on public issues in the United States.

As this issue has returned to the front burner of public policy consideration within the American body politic, the Jewish community and other concerned groups, Prof. Marshall J. Breger of the Columbus School of Law, Catholic University of America, Washington, D.C., and Dr. David M. Gordis, Director of the Wilstein Institute of Jewish Policy Studies, determined to create a non-partisan forum for its reconsideration. Each approached the question from his own unique perspective while sharing a concern that the rhetoric of debate not obscure the significant issues to be considered and analyzed.

This goal was realized in a conference held on May 19, 1997 at the Columbus School of Law and co-sponsored by it and the Wilstein Institute of Jewish Policy Studies, with Prof. Breger and Dr. Gordis as its co-convenors. The participants reflected a broad spectrum of political, educational and religious approaches and the program attempted to place the current discussion within the context of historical perspectives. This volume offers the record of those presentations and round table discussions. Several additional papers germane to the issue have been added, mostly reflecting specific Jewish communal concerns, as well as a group of papers analyzing the implications of the decision of the United States Supreme Court in the matter of *Agostini v. Felton*. That decision was handed down by the Court shortly after the conference and the editors of this volume felt that its implications might be significant for this ongoing discussion. A group of eminent legal scholars was asked to analyze the decision and assess its relevance to the question at hand.

The purpose of this volume is to present a range of views and perspectives, not definitive answers. The product of many hands and minds, with as many opinions, it reflects the potential for civil and mutually respectful discussion of public issues that is often enflamed by the passion of ideological commitments.

Events during the period from the time of the conference to the actual publication of this volume, including the June, 1998 decision of the Wisconsin Supreme Court regarding the Milwaukee Parental Choice Program, and the announcement by a group of business leaders that they have pledged to raise two hundred million dollars for a national non-governmental voucher program, as well as ongoing attention in the press and other forums for discussion of public policy issues, indicate to us the relevance and continuing timeliness of the material presented in this volume. We hope that it will make a significant contribution to illuminating this discussion.

The convenors of the conference express their gratitude to Bernard Dobranski, Dean of the Columbus School of Law, Catholic University of America, and to Robert Destro, Professor of Law and Director of the Interdisciplinary Program in Law and Religion at Columbus School of Law, for their encouragement and efforts on behalf of the original conference and in the preparation of this volume; to the staff members of the two sponsoring institutions, whose efforts contributed to the success of our conference; and to Bernard Barsky, who worked closely with me in bringing this volume to publication and whose editorial skills have contributed significantly its quality.

Acknowledgments

Partial funding for our work in this area was provided by:

Anonymous

The Avi Chai Foundation

J. Morton Davis

The Milton and Rose Friedman Foundation

Michael David Epstein

Dr. Paul S. Friedman

Philip Hixon

Shelly Kamins

The Catholic University of America's Columbus School of Law and the Susan and David Wilstein Institute of Jewish Policy Studies gratefully acknowledge these individuals and organizations for their generous support.

School Vouchers – A Sympathetic View

Marshall J. Breger

We are entering a period of ferment in the field of education. Everywhere, the old approaches to public education are being rethought and refought.

Recent years have seen the dissipation of the traditional deference given to experts in the public school system with a concomitant revival of the notion of parental control. We have also seen a shift away from the public school hegemony over primary and secondary education. The changes include "reconstituted" schools, where teachers have to reapply for their positions depending on the quality of school results; charter schools, where innovative, often parent-driven educational centers have been set up in at least 22 states with minimal control by educational bureaucracies and teachers; alternative schools, (a New York City variant which allows "charter" schools in all but name), intra- and inter-district attendance policies, whereby pupils can choose any public school, whether within their own district or (as in the Massachusetts public schools) in a neighboring district.

Further, we have seen a growing functional permeability between the public and private sector. Some communities have brought in private companies to manage their schools. States provide various forms of assistance to private school students, ranging from bus transportation costs to reimbursement for required testing and school textbook aid. Efforts have been made in Milwaukee and Cleveland to support school voucher programs. And further along the continuum, recourse to home schooling, while still unusual, is no longer considered bizarre.

Many of these innovations have been accepted by the educational community with only a minimum of complaint. Others have been fought over vociferously. Perhaps the most contentious issue on the educational reform agenda is school vouchers. It is on this issue that supporters of a public school monopoly, teachers unions, and partisans of strict church-state separation have seemingly drawn their line in the sand. School vouchers then, are more than an educational experiment, they are a pennant in the culture wars.

To some extent the fear of vouchers reflects a desire to build ever higher the so-called "wall of separation" between church and state. The argument is that support of parochial schools through vouchers results in "excessive entanglement" of the state in religious affairs. And it is often asserted that the intent of the voucher schemes is actually to aid and promote religion. Voucher supporters counter by arguing that the state remains "neutral" toward religion in a voucher program, since the money goes to parents who can choose to use it at a public, private, or parochial school. And moreover, there are other reasons to support vouchers than a covert infusion of funds to religious institutions. These include promoting parental empowerment and injecting competition into failing inner-city public schools. The recent Wisconsin State Supreme Court decision in *Jackson v. Benson* (1998), suggests that the constitutional cloud over vouchers may soon be lifted and the issue can be considered on its merits.

Nor should one fail to notice an interesting subtext that can be read beneath the religious issue, namely a dislike of private schools whatever their stripe. To be sure, the Supreme Court rejected the notion of a public school monopoly over seventy years ago, in *Pierce v. Society of Sisters* (1925). And so public school enthusiasts, thus deprived of the ability to outlaw all private schools, talk around the issue. But their hearts' desire is clear. Indeed, when the state of Maryland was considering providing textbooks to private schools as a form of state support, both the teachers unions and the Jewish Federations came out in full force against such assistance. They opposed this state assistance even though it is done in over 20 states and is generally accepted as constitutional under present Supreme Court jurisprudence. The Federations felt that any government support for private schools *must necessarily* imply a diminution of state support for public schools.

All this is unfortunate, for it has kept many constituencies from examining the concept of school vouchers on its merits. In particular, the symbolic freight of the voucher concept has inhibited the Jewish community, notwithstanding its newfound recognition of the importance of day schools in ensuring Jewish continuity, from looking objectively at vouchers as a public policy question.

The papers in this volume review a wide range of issues related to school choice, including a focus on these issues from a Jewish perspective. Because the participants as well as the editors of this volume may have different views on the constitutionality and desirability of vouchers, the book considers a broad range of issues from many points of view, including the key role of Jewish day schools in sustaining Jewish continuity; the desperate financial challenge of paying for such day schools; the needs of poor inner-city students and the advantages to them of parental choice. This book also looks at the public policy arguments against supporting vouchers, including the alleged weakening of the public schools, the need for some forum like public schools to teach common civic values, and the fear that voucher schemes will spawn schools sponsored by extremist political and religious organizations with views inimical to those of the Jewish community.

Jewish Continuity

From a Jewish public policy perspective, the main argument for school vouchers is a practical one—a belief that they will foster Jewish continuity. The 1990 National Jewish Population Survey, sponsored by the Council of Jewish Federations, has shown fairly conclusively that the strongest indicator of Jewish continuity is the intensity of an individual's Jewish education. While some have suggested that this need can be met by Jewish summer camps and afternoon programs, most agree that the formative Jewish experience for adolescents in today's aggressively secular society is a Jewish day school, of whatever denomination. That is why we have seen a remarkable growth in day schools connected to the Conservative and Reform movements in Judaism, a percentage growth greater than that of Orthodox schools. Vouchers, it is argued, will both allow parents who could not otherwise afford to do so to send their children to Jewish schools or, in some cases, (where schools may raise tuition in light of this newfound "subsidy") provide a supplement to improve their educational "product." (It must be noted in fairness, however, that voucher opponents argue that the proposed sums involved, $1500–$3000 per child, are too small to make the difference for a family considering a Jewish school.)

Finances

The problem, of course, is financing. While there has been considerable talk about the organized Jewish community increasing its commitment to day schools, the fiscal requirements of going it alone are indeed awesome. Marvin Schick in this volume has detailed the coming fiscal crisis of Jewish day schools and has pointed up the need for substantial infusion of funds from public or private sources. Over 200,000 Jewish students now attend day schools and even without expected growth, parental tuition alone will not do the job.

Recently, there have been calls for an extraordinary commitment to day school support from local Jewish Federations. The question often ignored by voucher opponents, however, is whether private philanthropy, no matter how munificent, has sufficiently deep pockets to meet the need. After all is said about the necessity for redoubling the communal effort, it is unlikely that the community can support an educational system on its own. Perhaps some more rigorous empirical study, or recourse to the Catholic experience, would be of assistance in understanding this issue.

Most of the voucher debate has been the constitutionality and wisdom of government subsidized vouchers. There has been little discussion of the use of private vouchers in the Jewish community. Private voucher schemes are programs set up by private philanthropy to offer vouchers or scholarships to children to go to the school of their choice. While private voucher programs have caught on in the general community—they exist now in some 32 cities, with over 14,000 children receiving some form of private voucher aid—Jewish communal charities have made little use of them. But consider:

- In New York City, the School Choice Scholarship Foundation, responding to a challenge by Cardinal O'Connor, provided 1300 scholarships to children to attend private, parochial or public schools, including Jewish day schools and yeshivas. There were over 22,500 applicants.
- In the District of Columbia, two philanthropists, Ted Forstmann and John Walton, have contributed $6 million to the Washington Scholarship Fund to provide 1000 scholarships to poverty level D.C. school children.
- An organization started by business leaders in San Antonio announced that they would provide $50 million over the next ten years for a voucher program that would allow poor children in one school district to opt for private schools.

Jewish philanthropy has approached this challenge in different ways. Federations make grants (often woefully insufficient) directly to day schools, not through parental choice. Michael Steinhardt has spearheaded a new foundation, Partnership for Excellence in Jewish Education, which offers challenge grants to build new day schools in unserved communities. (The Partnership began with an $18 million kitty provided by 12 donors.) George Hanus and the National Jewish Day School Scholarship Committee are leading a mass effort to raise a $300 million endowment fund that would pay full tuition for day school students in Chicago. The drive has urged all Jews to commit 5 percent of their estate to Jewish Education trust funds. This "Operation Jewish Education/the 5 Percent Plan" was recently endorsed by the Jewish Federation of Metropolitan Chicago, which pledged an additional 10 percent to any monies collected by individual day schools up to $30 million and agreed to assist in the administration of such day school endowment funds. While other Federations have not yet joined in, a similar effort in Los Angeles is led by Joseph Bobker, owner of the *Los Angeles Jewish Times*. Eschewing the trust fund approach, the Los Angeles effort would provide subsidies directly to day school parents.

In Seattle, the Samis Foundation conducted a survey to ascertain the "clearing price" above which parents would be less likely to pay for a yeshiva education for their child. Determining that sum to be about $3,000, one Seattle yeshiva set its tuition accordingly and Samis subsidized the rest. Student enrollment increased from 58 in 1995 to 76 in the 1997–98 school year. AVI CHAI, a Jewish foundation, established an experimental private voucher program in Atlanta and Cleveland in Spring 1998. The Foundation will provide a $3,000 voucher yearly for up to four years to students who *transfer into* a Jewish day school and who do not have siblings presently attending or who have previously attended such a school. The program serves Reform, Conservative, Orthodox, and community wide schools. While the program didn't begin until late summer, over forty students from Atlanta and over twenty from Cleveland participated. AVI CHAI has committed over one million dollars to this effort long term.

The growth of privately funded voucher schemes is to be applauded. But few would argue that private funding alone can meet the demand. And indeed, statements to that effect by Jewish leaders (like Robert Rifkind of the American Jewish Committee) strike one as a debater's thrust and not as a serious response to the question of how we pay for Jewish education.

Parental Control

As is clear from the pro-voucher contributions to this volume, a major rationale for the growth of interest in school vouchers nationally has been increased interest in parental empowerment. While Jewish parents have always been intensely concerned with their children's education—education is virtually a Jewish mother's gift of social mobility—the rhetoric of parental empowerment is not often used in Jewish voucher debates. Perhaps it is because of Jewish respect for the purported "expertise" of the educational establishment. Perhaps it is because Jewish parents exercise their "empowerment" all the time by putting their children in private or day schools, or by moving to better neighborhoods.

But there can be no doubt that parental control is very important to the Black and Hispanic poor in large inner-city school systems. For them, empowerment is a vital aspect of improving their lives and the lives of their children. For them, anything that leads to empowerment has the potential to increase the level of parental involvement. Studies indicate that increased parental involvement is likely the single most effective way of improving student performance.

The Needs of the Poor

Any ordinary citizen who looks at the school system in most urban environments knows that it has failed students. William Raspberry, an Afro-American syndicated columnist for the Washington Post, has written that he used to oppose vouchers because he feared they would take money and support from the public schools. But recently he concluded that if vouchers might save 10,000 school children from the inner-city, that would be 10,000 more than at present. If the choice is helping a few or helping no one, Raspberry is prepared to jump in. Indeed, polls make it clear that a majority of Blacks support school vouchers. Yet one of the most frequent anti-voucher arguments among Jewish leaders is still that vouchers will hurt the inner-city poor.

The Public School and Civic Virtue

Now that most American Jews have been successfully Americanized (with a vengeance, some would add), the role of the public school has been transmogrified into the incubator of common or civic values. This is Horace Mann's notion of a "common school" brought into the twentieth century.

It is difficult to know, though, what Jews mean by a common school. If they mean a school integrated by class and race, geographically based public schools often lack diversity of race and class. Indeed, Catholic schools, in general, are far more diverse than public schools (certainly suburban public schools) on race, class and, yes, on religion too.

It is likely that the term "common school" refers to the teaching of common values, or what we used to call, more quaintly, citizenship or civics. While it is correct that our society is fractionating and that our common values may be fraying, it is unfair to expect the public school system to repair the damage. That is a challenge for society at large. Indeed, the equation of vouchers with balkanization and the loss of civility and tolerance is empirically unproved and indeed implausible. I doubt people would call the Netherlands a country lacking in tolerance. Yet it has one of the most well-developed voucher programs in the world. Some would argue, as Professor Charles Glenn has done in *Choice of School in Six Nations*, that it has in fact increased civility. Furthermore, expanded school choice has also been accompanied by some degree of increasing political tolerance in Eastern Europe (again, see Charles Glenn, *Educational Freedom in Eastern Europe*.) I would be interested in examples where a voucher system has actually resulted in the "ungluing of mutual restraint and tolerance." I doubt that such examples exist.

The Fear of Extremism

One policy argument often advanced against vouchers is the concern that they would be used by groups generally viewed as inimical to Jews. Thus, in an American Jewish Committee meeting in Boston, former Congressman Father Drinan (D-MA) struck gold when he repeatedly pointed to the Christian Coalition as a group whose parochial schools would proliferate under a voucher scheme. And more pointedly, Martin Kaplan of the American Jewish Committee has asked, "What is to prevent parents using these funds to send their children to Nation of Islam Schools? Or Branch Davidian Schools? Or Church of Scientology? Nothing of course."

This is a serious policy objection—although not a legal one, but it is ultimately not persuasive. It can be met, however, at two levels. First, even Nation of Islam parents should have choices. If they want to bring up their children in their religion, that is their parental prerogative. More relevant, however, the state has the right to regulate set standards for schools that receive vouchers. Indeed, even now they regulate private schools for substantive content before certifying them for granting diplomas.

Now I recognize that government bureaucrats hate to investigate religious institutions. It's messy and rarely makes friends, let alone influences people. Still, it is up to the various state Departments of Education to undertake these tasks and ensure minimal educational standards in private schools.

The End of Public School?

The teachers unions argue that vouchers are part of an effort to destroy the public school system. While it cannot be denied that there are some conservatives who want to get the state out of the school business, or as they put it, "separate schools from state," the goal of a voucher system is certainly not to destroy the public school. But it does aim to lift what has effectively been a public school monopoly on education.

The viability of the public school system has little to do with vouchers. In upper middle class areas where public schools are often first-rate, parents will likely still choose public education. Only in the inner-city, where schools have failed their students, and among religious groups with strong needs to provide an integrative spiritual and cultural identity, are vouchers likely to significantly increase the numbers who switch to private schooling.

The anti-voucher groups advance with certitude two propositions for which they have so far failed to provide supporting empirical evidence. The first is that money for vouchers will in some way undermine public education. But given that inflationñadjusted spending on education in the U.S. increased by 50 percent in 1974 and 1991, reaching an all time high at $300 billion last year, it is hard to see any diminution of funds for public education in the offing.

The second unproven proposition is that if parochial schools are better, this is only because they are able to "cherry pick" students in a way that public schools cannot. And yet, while it may be true that parochial schools do have high disciplinary standards, they are still likely to achieve more racial, ethnic and class integration than the public schools. So even if these concerns need to be respected, they can hardly be said to dispose of the matter, for it is certainly possible to imagine voucher systems that address them.

Conclusion

Last year the Jewish Council on Public Affairs (JCPA) began a one-year reexamination of the Jewish community position on school vouchers. JCPA set up a task force to revisit the issue, and a significant portion of their efforts were encompassed in the conference from which this collection of materials is drawn.

In February 1998 at its annual meeting in Ft. Lauderdale, JCPA voted to reaffirm its traditional position. (Its voucher policy statement is included in the third section of this volume.) JCPA aside, however, there can be little doubt that the ferment in educational issues that has enveloped the general community is continuing and will not ignore Jewish communal needs. Already local Jewish communities are increasing support for day schools, and leading philanthropists are creating "trusts" to support day school development. And while we are not yet at the point where day school education is understood to be a responsibility of the entire Jewish community in the same way as aid to Israel or aid to the elderly, we are moving rapidly in that direction.

While the contributors to this volume reflect different views of the propriety of vouchers, one hopes that all would accept debate in this area as useful. Unfortunately this is not always the case. For many in the educational establishment, discussion and experimentation around the subject of vouchers is *verboten*. This is the case even though a June 1998 Gallup poll showed a majority of Americans favoring vouchers Most Jewish groups oppose even limited experiments such as those proposed by Senator Joseph Lieberman, who would support a voucher program limited to inner-city school districts for a three year study period. Vouchers should not be the policy orphan of educational reform. The Jewish community should not let ideological blinders impede discussion of its own and this country's future educational needs.

School Vouchers—A Skeptical View

David M. Gordis

It was once suggested that for every complex and difficult question there is a simple and elegant answer—and it's wrong. The complex of issues relating to education and school vouchers—historical, political, ideological, economic, philosophical and pragmatic—raises profound questions. They relate to public, private, and religious (particularly, but not uniquely, Jewish and Catholic) schools. There are few if any simple and elegant answers, and that includes school vouchers, the subject of this volume and the conference that gave birth to it. That very complexity, and the desire to penetrate it and shed new light on these issues, led the Columbus School of Law and the Wilstein Institute of Jewish Policy Studies to undertake the conference held in May of 1997. The conference evolved under the joint leadership of Professor Marshall Breger of the Columbus School of Law and myself, as Director of The Susan and David Wilstein Institute of Jewish Policy Studies.

It was the intention of the sponsors of this conference to break with some earlier rhetorical patterns that have characterized much of the public debate on these issues. Opponents and proponents of school vouchers have tended to dismiss their adversaries as ideologues incapable of dealing with issues in ways which responded to their complexity. Conservative proponents accused Jewish opponents of vouchers of the "crimes" of liberalism and secularism, as though that was enough to discredit real concerns. Opponents dismissed proponents in similar fashion, demonizing them and suggesting nefarious hidden agendas underlying their positions. This conference set out to break that pattern of debate: it aimed for civility and substantive engagement with the real issues of concern to both sides. It brought together a broad spectrum of discussants, politically, religiously, racially and ideologically diverse. While ideological cant is not entirely lacking from these presentations, the dominant tone is civil, substantive and serious, and demonstrates an awareness that this is not an easy or unproblematic call from either side.

It should be possible to move quickly beyond broad ideological strokes, and by and large that was accomplished. Legal issues are explored thoroughly in these presentations; they are real but not decisive. While there is general support for the separation of church and state, most respondents agree that the separation is not and never has been absolute and that ways of dealing with legal challenges to vouchers can be found if that emerges as the best path to follow.

Other issues are more difficult. Is it clear that vouchers really work with a cross-section population of the most troubled schools? The evidence so far is inconclusive. What would be the impact of siphoning off these voucher funds from public schools? The issue is not "protecting the public school monopoly on education," as my friend and colleague Marshall Breger puts it. That monopoly does not exist. We do have private schools and parochial and religious schools. Arguments are made on both sides concerning the economic impact on public schools. The vast majority of this country's public schools are providing quality education and are shaping a pattern of intergroup relationships that is essential for the success of American pluralism. They need and deserve continued support. How will the reduced costs of lower student enrollment in the public schools balance against the reduced support resulting from resources being channeled to the voucher program and ultimately to private schools of various kinds? The issue of "quality control" is a serious one despite dismissive statements about the problem. No suggestions were made as to how vouchers would prevent public support for destructive and sociopathic ideological schools. What way could be found to establish governmental standards to prevent public funding of racist, anti-Semitic, anti-democratic or other objectionable schools without bringing about unacceptable government entanglement in religion?

The challenge to provide for high quality Jewish education to ensure the creative vitality and continuity of Jewish life is profound. It requires a concerted and focused response. But whose responsibility is Jewish education for Jewish continuity? Surely it lies primarily with the Jewish community itself, which is beginning to meet that challenge with increasing resources. Day schools are vital. So are other forms of formal and non-formal education. A preoccupation with one educational form may be useful rhetoric but it is not sound public policy. That debate, too, must be an internal Jewish community debate. The pattern of separation of church and state which has evolved in the United States is not sacrosanct for ideological reasons; it can be adjusted if there are good reasons to adjust it. But to alter that pattern in order to use public funds for purposes of Jewish continuity (and Catholic and Muslim and Buddhist continuity!) would imperil a system that has achieved unprecedented success for religion in this country. That system has provided religious groups the freedom to create flourishing and independent institutions and to compete for adherents, and it has made America into the most religious country in the Western world. Tampering with a pattern of separation which has proven so successful carries with it great risk; and so far the evidence has been insufficient to justify that risk.

It should also be noted that some putative alliances may dissolve when specifics of a voucher plan are put on the table. For example, middle class Jews who have expectations that vouchers will have a significant impact on tuition charged at Jewish day schools will be disappointed by a voucher plan that is targeted specifically to inner-city and other disadvantaged schools, which constitute the most compelling pro-voucher argument. Those expectations are challenged by some of the pro-voucher Jewish voices in this volume.

My reading of the contributions to this volume suggests the wisdom of the position of the Jewish Council on Public Affairs (JCPA). Reaffirming their opposition to the wholesale adoption of vouchers, the JCPA and many other Jewish community agencies are strengthening their efforts to help build an effective Jewish educational structure through the allocation of greater Jewish community resources. They are successfully encouraging major philanthropists to invest more heavily in Jewish education, while reiterating their support for public education and endorsing further study of the issue and experiments with alternative forms of public education including charter and magnet schools. Approaches to the application of public funds to components of private and religious education which have been ruled acceptable should continue to be pursued. Until more convincing arguments and evidence for a major shift in position favoring wide support of school vouchers is adduced, however, the present position of the Jewish community is wise and appropriate.

This volume is not meant to end the discussion; on the contrary, it is meant to contribute to the discussion and encourage further reflection. It is our hope that as we articulate our positions with vigor and conviction we do not lose the capacity to hear the voices of those who disagree. They do so with no less conviction than ours, no less intelligence than ours, and no less eagerness to find the best policy directions for our country, for our people, and for all people.

Section One:

Implications of School Vouchers for Public Schools and for American Society

INTRODUCTION

Jay Greene

Several papers of this section focus on some actual experiments in school choice now taking place—in Milwaukee, Cleveland and New York—and the effects of those experiments on academic achievement and racial integration. The consequences of school choice, and people's perceptions about those consequences, are really the heart of the school choice debate. The constitutionality of school choice which includes religiously-affiliated schools will probably soon be decided by the U.S. Supreme Court now that the Wisconsin Supreme Court has affirmed the use of vouchers at religious schools (*Jackson v. Benson* (1998)). The Wisconsin Court, closely following the reasoning in last year's U.S. Supreme Court decision on the use of Title 1 instruction for poor students in religious schools (*Agostini v. Felton* (1997)), argued that the Milwaukee school choice program could include religious schools as long as the selection of a religious or secular school was a matter of individual parental choice and not government coercion.

Given the presumption that the constitutionality of school choice which includes religious school options may well soon be a moot question, our attention should turn to the issues addressed in this section: whether choice is desirable public policy and whether it has the political support to be adopted. The contributors to this section offer some differing perspectives but also share a good amount of common ground.

A number of presenters comment on the extent and value of the evidence available so far on the effects of school choice. Jeffrey Henig worries that the current evidence is sparse and over-interpreted. Martin Plax similarly argues that the experience with school choice in Cleveland has been less than conclusive. In my remarks I agree that we do not have definitive evidence, but the initial results from the school choice programs in Milwaukee and Cleveland are encouraging and are certainly sufficient to justify additional and expanded experiments. Chester Finn notes that there are now over thirty publicly or privately funded school choice programs underway, many of which are being systematically monitored to obtain evidence about their effects on academic achievement.

Henig also raises concerns about the effects of school choice on integration and the idea of the common school. State Representative Polly Williams of Milwaukee argues that the primary concern of African-American parents is the quality of education, not integration, and that choice is the vehicle for improving quality. Like Henig, I too am interested in integration and the common school, but I report that an analysis of data collected by the U.S. Department of Education suggests that private schools, based on voluntary association, are actually better racially integrated than public schools, which tend to replicate and reinforce racially segregated housing patterns. Former Congressman Floyd Flake of New York, like Polly Williams, observes that bussing to achieve integration has been disproportionately burdensome on African-Americans, but without producing the promised improvements in school quality.

Several contributors point out that school choice already exists for those with the financial resources to purchase a private education or move to higher quality suburban school districts. Finn pointedly suggests that many Jewish organizations may be hypocritical to oppose giving poor, inner-city minorities the opportunity to choose a school, while most Jews themselves enjoy the ability to select the school that is best for their children. In Cleveland, according to Plax, mainstream Jewish organization have opposed school choice plans even though virtually no Jews reside any longer within the city limits of Cleveland, having already relocated to better suburban school districts.

In contrast to this mainstream Jewish opposition, the Catholic establishment, represented here by the Most Reverend James T. McHugh, Bishop of Camden, New Jersey, strongly supports vouchers. Bishop McHugh describes Catholic schools as a crucial alternative for the largely non-Catholic inner-city communities that many of those schools serve. Catholic schools already perform this function even without vouchers, but vouchers, he argues, would make their task much easier. It is apparent that, with mainstream Jewish organizations coming down on one side of this question, and the Catholic Church and Democratic, African-American leaders like Polly Williams and Floyd Flake coming down on the other, the issue of school vouchers does not neatly divide people along traditional political lines.

Whether school choice will have positive consequences or the political support to be adopted more broadly is still not perfectly clear. Henig points out that polls show most Americans are satisfied with their public schools. The dissatisfaction, however, seems to be strongest among the poor and racial minorities who currently have access to the fewest educational choices. The greatest support for school choice exists among these groups and the least support among white suburbanites. Whether the types of cross-racial and bi-partisan coalitions that were formed to pass school choice legislation in Wisconsin and Ohio can be assembled elsewhere is open to question. But once the U.S. Supreme Court finally settles the constitutionality of the issue, hopefully in the next year, the efficacy of school choice and the strength of the political coalitions backing it will finally be put to the test.

School Choice in the History of Education in the United States

Jeffrey Henig

In addition to a whirlwind chronology of school choice, I want to highlight two points. The first is to address the question why there was (as I would argue) a resurgence of this school choice/school voucher notion in the mid-to-late 1980s. It was an idea that had been around in a fairly well-developed form at least since the late 1950s or early 1960s, as formulated by Milton Friedman. But it sort of fizzled around and bumped around for a long time without broad impact on public policy. Why did it come back into the mainstream of the public agenda pretty much coincident with Ronald Reagan's second term of office?

The second issue I want to deal with in this chronology is the distinction which I find useful between school choice *in theory*—as an abstract formulation often based on market principles—and school choice *in practice*—as a pragmatic tool for public officials to achieve specific goals in specific contexts.

Let me start with the original idea of school choice. The story here is of an intriguing theory with relatively few takers. University of Chicago economist Milton Friedman laid out the vision most prominently in his book *Capitalism and Freedom*. Friedman argued that public schools had essentially become lazy monopolies. They had no incentive to improve the product they were delivering because parents, basically, were trapped into geographically defined zones of attendance. They could not choose their public school, and even if they opted out of the public schools altogether, they were dunned by government and forced to pay for the system. So the public school bureaucracies were free to deliver a mediocre product. Friedman's solution in the areas of schools, as elsewhere, was to introduce dramatically stronger market forces. He proposed to do that on the demand side by converting the public revenues that were going directly to school districts into vouchers that would go to parents, who would be free to shop around for the best school. On the supply side, he proposed to radically deregulate what we might call the "basic necessities" of what a school provides. This would allow entrepreneurs and concerned others to form schools without being restricted dramatically by regulations concerning the school nurse, the ratio of bathrooms to students, specific curriculum requirements, and the like.

As far as I can tell, there really wasn't an immediate response to the school part of Friedman's book. I went back and read a lot of book reviews and, mostly, they ignored it. Gradually the idea of school vouchers did take hold, but it did so primarily in the academic community. It was something that academics and scholars and policy analysts liked to talk about. In 1971, one observer went so far as to say that "on the intellectual circuit, vouchers are one of the hottest things going." But the story of indifference or even hostility toward vouchers in the public policy realm is told, I think, most clearly by the experience of the federal government—specifically, the Office of Economic Opportunity—which tried quite aggressively in the early 70s to find school districts around the country willing to experiment systematically with a voucher proposal. In spite of offering federal support to such an experiment, and occasionally finding local districts that were interested in talking about it, they had a very difficult time getting any district to sign on the dotted line. In the end, the only district that did—Alum Rock, California—did so only for a much attenuated experiment in school choice that did not involve private schools but was limited to public schools.

Now why did this idea of a true market-based school voucher system, which percolated in the academic community, fizzle in its influence on public policy? The conventional explanation blames bureaucratic resistance—resistance within the education community. There is something to this. The teachers' organizations certainly opposed school voucher experiments. They told a congressional committee that the purpose of the Office of Economic Opportunity in its pursuit of this experiment "has been redirected into an ill-conceived attempt to reprivatize our social services." And remember, the teacher's unions were even stronger then than now.

But I believe that the role of the unions and the education community in blocking school vouchers is much overstated. The reluctance to take on a market-based voucher proposal was much more widespread and deep-rooted than that.

Public officials and citizens, when they had a chance to discuss the specifics of proposals, found them easy to resist, and did so for a number of reasons. Let me just list some that I think were important.

First, many Americans (at least at that time period) were not convinced that there was a serious problem with American education. It was the case then, as now, that when Americans were polled about the quality of public schools in their own communities, there was a remarkably high percentage who thought the schools were doing an adequate job.

Second, there was a deeply rooted concern about the church-state issue, and uncertainty about how the courts would deal with any voucher plan that included parochial schools.

Third, I would argue that there is a culture of pragmatism that characterizes the American public—a skepticism towards abstract theory and a wariness about attempts to move ideas from the ivory tower, or from economics textbooks, into the real world.

Fourth, I think Americans, by and large, have had mixed experience with markets, and they are ambivalent in their endorsement of the principle that the private markets that they experience (their local supermarket or gas station) are as responsive to their needs and interests as market principles might suggest they should be.

Fifth, there is the power of a counter-vision, a counter-vision that was, I think, stronger and more clearly articulated then than it is now. That is a vision of public school, the common school, as a vehicle for social integration in a country that identifies itself as a melting pot. Public schools were seen positively as a way to bring into one forum, one publicly guided forum, people of diverse ethnic and economic background and to provide them with a common education that would build a public, national identity that supersedes fragmented forces in the country.

And last (at least that I'm going to mention), the idea of school choice carried with it some baggage—baggage in terms of the history of how school choice had been used recently in the American educational system, and specifically in response to *Brown vs. Board of Education.*

This brings me to my second broad focus, which relates to the distinction between school choice in practice and school choice as an idea. By practice, I mean the pragmatic uses of choice to pursue the goals of public officials or influential interest groups. After *Brown vs. Board of Education,* school choice emerged most significantly in Deep South states that saw choice and vouchers as vehicles for evading the consequences of that decision. Choice and vouchers were tools in the massive resistance of many Deep South school districts. Some districts and some states passed legislation enacting voucher systems. They thought that by converting public support into vouchers, and allowing parents to go to nominally private schools, they would not have to desegregate because the Brown decision applied only to public schools. The courts eventually outlawed that practice. But in the 60s that history was fresh in people's minds. I think it's not fresh in people's minds now.

A second way that school choice evolved in practice, quietly and not tied to broad theories, was as a safety valve. In many school districts, school officials over the years gradually found it useful to put into place at least limited choice plans, not always publicly announced, as a way to handle angry parents—parents who have fights with particular teachers and principals, or parents who felt that the curriculum at their local assigned school was not appropriate for their child. Many school districts throughout the country have used choice selectively, in limited and sometimes discriminatory ways, but nonetheless as a way to "take the heat off" them over time.

A third type of school choice in practice relates to alternative education. Here there is a history going back at least to the Progressive era early in the 20th century of public schools that offer some kind of alternative curriculum. Sometimes these alternative schools were based on innovative pedagogical philosophy; sometimes they were designed to deal with troubled students of one kind or another. But there's a history of these schools in many cities—academic schools like Bronx High School of Science in New York—that provided a form of choice. Students were not assigned to them. There are said to be roughly (although I don't know that these counts are particularly reliable) about 2,200 public schools that fit this model of alternative education based on a form of school choice.

And finally, there is the practice of magnet schools providing a form of school choice. I would argue that this is the most important example. Magnet schools began to be adopted by a number of school districts in the early 70s—sometimes as an alternative to busing, sometimes as a complement to busing—as a way to minimize the degree of mandatory reassignment. Through magnet schools a school district may offer a variety of special curricula—French immersion, math, science, gifted and talented, whatever—to make schools (often in minority neighborhoods) more attractive to white parents. The federal government has provided financial support in many instances for local school districts to use magnets as part of desegregation efforts. Magnet schools are now in place widely around the country.

This is where idea and practice come together. I believe that the resurgence of the school choice and voucher idea in the mid-to-late 80s is related to the Republican administration's decision to adopt magnet schools as a stalking horse for the more extreme choice proposals they favored. Ronald Reagan and Secretary Bennett were not successful during Reagan's first term in bringing voucher proposals all the way through Congress. As in the past, people liked the idea, and many people talked about it. But it just didn't have the political muscle to get through. In January 1988, Ronald Reagan went out to a magnet school in Prince George's County, Svitland High School, and made a speech that I think was significant as a turning point on this issue. It was presented at the time as a sign of collapse on the part of the Reagan Administration, a backing away from private school choice and an endorsement of a much weaker vision of public school choice. Reagan called the magnets of Prince George's County a great experiment. He linked them to the concept of choice, but by doing so—and by acknowledging that public school efforts were significant—he took a step that many pro-choice advocates saw as a step backwards. But I think this was a classic case of one step backwards in order to make two steps forward.

By linking the abstract theory of school choice to the practice already out there in many school districts, the proponents of school choice accomplished at least three things:

First, they were able to point to an empirical record that demonstrated (or at least they argued that it demonstrated) that school choice was feasible. It was not just an ivory tower theory. It already exists out there in many public school districts.

Second, they were able to claim that the track record of those schools showed that school choice is not only doable, but is consistent with goals of racial integration and class integration. In other words, this was an inoculation, if you will, against the charge that school choice was necessarily linked to the history of massive resistance in the South. By pointing to magnet schools which were integrated—and more integrated in many respects than other public schools—they were able to say choice and integration were compatible.

Third, proponents of school choice could now begin to claim, based on empirical data, that school choice had positive effects on academic performance. In fact, many of the magnet schools out there had experienced improvements in test scores, although I would argue that these were due primarily to changes in the student bodies—to the particular students attracted to the magnet schools—rather than to the power of choice itself. But nonetheless, the claim was made that school choice was associated with improved performance.

Now, I have a lot of things that I could say and would say if I had more time, about this interpretation of the evidence. I would raise questions about whether the evidence really is as it was presented. My own argument is that even now, what we know about the consequences of school choice is quite limited, that good studies are rare, and that most of what is discussed is anecdotal and doesn't control for important factors. And I would also argue, in particular, that the generalization from the kinds of choice out there—publicly defined, publicly implemented school choice as actually practiced—the generalization from that toward support for more abstract, more extreme market-based proposals is highly problematic.

These issues aside, I will try to wrap things up by saying something about the practice of school choice in the post-Reagan era, and then make a couple of quick conclusions. First, since the Reagan Administration, school choice, at least within public school context, has continued to expand. It has expanded at the insistence of some state legislatures, which have passed open enrollment proposals allowing students to move across district boundaries. It has expanded in a few cases (specifically, two major ones that we'll be discussing later, Milwaukee and Cleveland) in more dramatic voucher type forms. And it has expanded in a lot of quiet ways, where schools have used choice to discretely modify enrollment policies as a political compromise to relieve heat on them, or to accommodate dissatisfied parents. A recent survey by the National Center for Education Statistics found that, when parents were asked whether they had exercised choice, almost 20 percent said they chose the school their children attended, and another 39 percent said schools had influenced where they chose to live. So a high percentage of Americans, at least when asked now, believe or assert that they have the option to choose their children's school. More of those parents who said they chose their school were in public schools than were in private schools. 10.9 percent attended public schools of choice compared to 8.8 percent who attended private school. So public school choice, at least according to this survey, is more extensive than private school choice.

Now, two concluding observations based on my reading of history. I think the resurgence of the idea of school vouchers is not attributable to a broad rejection of the vision of common school or of the legitimate role of government and public authority. Nor is it the result of the broad public's conversion to market principles. I do believe the idea has been gaining inroads, but less because of its power to convince the public than because of three other things I'll mention briefly. First, there is a growing sense of frustration with the performance of public schools, especially given a sense that we need to compete better internationally. Second, there is the misleading impression that choice experiments to date can reassure us that market-based voucher plans would not be a serious threat to racial and social integration. And third, there is a failure on the part of those who are still committed to public institutions to provide an updated vision of a common school. I mean a real, positive rationale for why we might want to be wary of embracing a market model.

My concluding observation is that the history of school choice as actually practiced shows that choice is best understood and most accepted by the American public, and is most useful, when it is seen as a tool. Like a hammer or other tool, choice can be used for good or for ill. It depends on who is using it, and for what particular goals. Choice in this sense, as a tool, means not thinking of choice as an alternative to having government define our educational policies. Rather, it means thinking of choice as a tool of government. School choice depends on good government to structure it in ways that are equitable and consistent with other publicly defined goals.

THE MILWAUKEE EXPERIMENT

The Editors

One of the speakers at our May 1997 conference, school choice pioneer, Annette "Polly" Williams (Representative for the 10th District, Wisconsin State Assembly) moved many in the audience with her cogent and passionate presentation of her experience and her argument favoring vouchers as a remedy for the educational problems facing her constituents. Unfortunately, the text of her presentation is not available for publication.

Frustrated by the apparent lack of concern for the plight of Black, Hispanic, and native American children in Milwaukee's central core, Polly Williams and her coalition attempted a series of reforms designed to put parents in control. Several were tried, but all the alternatives except one—vouchers—left the Milwaukee Public School system and its teachers union in charge of the educational destiny of the children. From the coalition's perspective the existing inertia mitigated against a resolution of the issues.

In her view, a voucher program is a strategic option that poor families need:

"The main issue is education and that is where we have to build new paths to help low income families. We want low-income families to be able to do what families with money have already done, which is to take their children out of the public schools that aren't addressing the needs of their students. Many of you in this audience may have taken your own kids out of public schools and put them in Jewish day schools or other schools where you know that they are going to get the best education that you can give them. Or else you move into a nice neighborhood where there are fine public schools. Remember that low income families don't have these options and are stuck with the schools that everyone else has abandoned. The middle class, both white and Black, has basically left public education. What kind of message is being given to us? Obviously something is going on in the public schools that is not good for children. Why can't we allow low-income families to escape also?"

She then indicated how vouchers would be used under the Milwaukee plan. They were limited to low-income families, and a cap was set on income so that the plan would effect only 1500 out of 100,000 students in Milwaukee. The amount of the per student state aid that would be credited to the Milwaukee Public Schools would be available instead to those eligible parents so that they could select a school that had committed to the program. That school could only request and accept the amount of the voucher. If the regularly charged tuition was higher than the amount of the state's per student budget, the school would be obliged to accept the lower amount without assessing the parents any more. In short, they limited the family income level and, therefore, the number of eligible children and they restricted the program to the city of Milwaukee. It was also made non-sectarian. With these provisos they were able to get the enabling legislation passed by the state legislature.

The titanic political and judicial battles which Milwaukee's embrace of a voucher remedy have spawned illustrate the thorny issues at the heart of debates within the Black community and elsewhere concerning the wisdom and utility of "school choice" as a strategy for furthering the economic and social welfare of inner-city and rural children. Some worry that private schools supported by vouchers will be segregated along racial and religious lines. Others, like Polly Williams, take a more pragmatic view, and focus on the goal of integration over the long term. She noted:

"It is interesting that we as Black Americans are fighting for vouchers, which are usually viewed as something that racist white people sought in the South in order not to go to school with Black children. Some people still feel that way. There are also many Black people who do not support vouchers because of the way white people used them in the South to run from Black people. I keep telling them that it does not matter. Let them run if they do not want to go to school with us. We can have our own schools under the voucher program. We can set up our own schools and run them the way we want to. Why do they feel that chasing white folks is the ultimate for us? White people don't tell their kids that they have to sit next to our children in order to be important. So let those people who want to run, go and run. There are Black people, too, who like to chase white people, who want to be integrated and live next door to them and go to school with them. Let them! But for those of us who feel that the education of our children is more important than anything else we can do for them, we know that we get only one time around with our kids. If we miss it we don't get a second chance."

Tension developed among the original coalition members over the distinction which a Wisconsin state court drew between religiously sponsored schools and those sponsored by secular groups. Religious groups want the program to be all-inclusive while others are concerned that the general community-based schools (public or private) should be permitted to move ahead with a vouchers program for the benefit of the children.

On June 10, 1998, in a 4-2 ruling in *Jackson v. Benson*, the Wisconsin Supreme Court upheld the expanded Milwaukee Parental Choice Program. The Court found that a program allowing the use of public funds in religious institutions is permissible if (1) the program is neutral between religious and secular options, and (2) parents or children, rather than the government, direct the funds.

The Court further ruled under the Wisconsin Constitution that the program does not operate primarily for the "benefit" of religious schools but rather that the children are the beneficiaries. It dismissed all other claims, including the NAACP's claim that the program unconstitutionally segregates Milwaukee's schools. The respondents (that is to say the State of Wisconsin) still have the option to appeal to the U.S. Supreme Court, and are likely to do so. Because this decision addresses First Amendment issues, it could have impact upon cases pending before state supreme courts in Ohio, Vermont and Maine. One thing is certain, this process will change the educational choices available to the people of Milwaukee and other cities.

The Cleveland Experiment

Martin J. Plax

Part One

Representative Williams' passionate presentation of the Milwaukee plan, and her role in its legislative history, stands in contrast to what I shall say about the Cleveland Voucher Plan and the response to vouchers in the Jewish community in Cleveland. For the past twenty years I have been an advocate on legislative and judicial matters for The American Jewish Committee. In Cleveland the AJC also actively mediates community conflicts, including intra-Jewish conflicts. Some conflicts have involved differences over government policy. I negotiated with some of the government officials involved in the creation of the Cleveland Voucher Plan and had private discussions with them while the plan was being shaped. Finally, since 1966 I have, mostly part-time, taught political science at several universities. My presentation will be a report by an interested observer and a seeker of ways to mediate the conflict that currently exists over the issue of vouchers.

The idea of introducing vouchers in Ohio appears to have been first articulated publicly by Republican Governor George Voinovich, who, before becoming Governor, had been the Mayor of the City of Cleveland. While Mayor, he had been helpless to do anything to help an ailing Cleveland Public School System. By statute, the Mayor of the City of Cleveland is prevented from any activity involving the public schools. The responsibility for the system rests with an independently elected School Board, a structural arrangement that was the legacy of the Reform era. We can see now that it was naive to believe that such a structural arrangement could insulate education from politics.

The experience that Voinovich had as Mayor proved to be frustrating, so, in campaigning for the governorship, both in 1992 and more so in 1994, Voinovich positioned himself as "the education governor." With his encouragement, in 1993, while the Democrats were still in control of the State Legislature, separate bills were introduced by Republicans in both the Ohio

House and Senate. They were introduced to create the Ohio Scholarship Plan, which was the name given to the voucher plan. The bill would have set aside $25 million for pilot programs in three or four school districts. The participating public schools would not lose any state funding during the trial period, regardless of how many students transferred to private schools. After the trial period, however, those schools which suffered losses of students could lose money.

According to the Senate sponsors, the pilot program consisted of "scholarships for tutorial assistance." The sum allotted to each recipient would be $2500 and would be made available to students in public schools and in "alternative schools" as one of the sponsors described them. The argument made by one sponsor of the legislation was that poor parents do not have choices when it comes to the education of their children, whereas affluent parents do have choices, either to send their children to private schools, or to move to areas with good public schools.

In an effort to build grass-roots support for vouchers, an Akron, Ohio industrialist, David L. Brennan, a very close political friend of the governor, paid $20,000 of his personal funds to have a survey done of Ohio residents. A sample of 1401 people were polled. The results, which were published in many Ohio papers, showed that 29 percent of the sample were very supportive of a pilot voucher plan and 43 percent were "somewhat supportive." The attempt at building public support for such a plan, however, failed. Brennan, and a group he created, calling itself "Hope for Ohio's Children," met stiff opposition from state and local teachers unions and a coalition of organizations traditionally serving as watchdogs for violations of the separation of church and state.

Strong opposition in the state legislature also came from African-American representatives. One in particular, C. J. Prentiss, from Cleveland, opposed the voucher plan on the grounds that it would take the best students in the Cleveland public schools out of those schools, leaving within the system only the most problematic children. This would put even greater strains on a troubled school system. As a result, the two Democratically controlled houses of the state legislature failed to act on the proposals.

In 1994, when the Republicans took control of both houses of the U.S. Congress, they also took control of both houses of the Ohio legislature. It was then that the Cleveland voucher plan was introduced, not as a separate bill, but as part of the 1995–1997 biennial budget. Governor Voinovich had envisioned the voucher program as a test project in more than one school district, but House Republicans limited it to the Cleveland public schools. It was financed by deducting $5.25 million from the pool of state money earmarked as "disadvantaged pupil impact aid," aimed at children from families receiving welfare. Critics, including the editorial writers at The Plain Dealer, Cleveland's only daily newspaper, complained that the voucher pilot program had been snuck into the budget and was not being debated on its own merits. In spite of the criticism, the legislative tactic succeeded.

The voucher project was established in the context of one significant fact. Because the Cleveland school system had gone broke, a federal district judge had ordered that the district be put under the control of the State Superintendent of Public Instruction. This decision took away all control of the schools of the locally elected school board. Thus, when the pilot project was created for the city of Cleveland, the Ohio Department of Education was formally responsible for creating the application procedure and the selection criteria for both students applying for vouchers and for schools applying for authorization to be recipients of the students with vouchers.

Initially, the program was created for students in kindergarten through grade 3. Provisions were made to expand the program in the following year to include an additional 3,000 children, K–4. The project provided that 50 percent of the vouchers had to be given to students who were enrolled in the public schools. Whether the "scholarship" students in the public schools remained in those schools was a matter left up to their parents. If the money was allocated to a starting point, it did not have to remain there.

Of the other 50 percent of the vouchers, they could be given to students in "alternative" schools. Included in this category were public schools in the suburbs immediately adjacent to the city of Cleveland, although none of them applied for such status. Also included in this category were sectarian private schools. All schools were required to meet state minimum standards for chartered non-public schools that had been put into effect on July 1, 1992. Registered private schools were allowed to specify the number of spaces available for "scholarship" students, with the understanding that preference must be given to low-income students.

In the first year of the experiment, 6000 students in the Cleveland schools, from kindergarten through third grade, applied for vouchers. Of those 6,000 applicants, 1,994 were selected, by lottery, and provided with vouchers worth 90 percent, or $2,250, of the $2,500 voucher limit, or the actual tuition of the private school, whichever was less. Plans for 1997 were to pay tuition for an additional 3,100 Cleveland students in the next two years.

As a result of the voucher plan, new alternative schools were created. A *Plain Dealer* story reported on two such schools: one, The Hope Academy Central, is a non-religious school financed by David Brennan. It is housed in the former Our Lady of Lourdes Catholic School. It has 272 students from households where the average income is $6,500. The other was Mount

Pleasant Christian School, which is on the far east side of Cleveland and which was purchased by the Cathedral Church of God and Christ in 1994. Of its 200 students in K through 8, 133 receive vouchers. The school was reported to be transformed into a K through 5 in the fall, with an expected enrollment of 250.

The *Plain Dealer* story, headlined "Vouching for School Choice," reported on two families who had received vouchers. In one instance, the story said, "a tuition voucher helped (Pamela) Balard change from a failing student in the Cleveland public schools to a pupil with As and Bs at Hope Central Academy, a non-religious school the voucher program created and supports." (In the other case, the story reported on a family with ten children who used the money "to buy a van so they could travel together for the first time." Only later did the story report that five of their children were already attending Our Lady of Good Counsel, a Catholic school in their neighborhood, and that the vouchers paid for the tuition of two of those children.)

As soon as the budget passed, the voucher plan was the subject of a legal challenge. In August, 1996 a Common Pleas judge in Franklin County (Columbus) upheld the constitutionality of the program. But on May 1, 1997, by a 3-0 vote, the Ohio Court of Appeals rejected the state officials' argument that the program is *not* intended to advance religion but to give poor children in the Cleveland schools a chance to choose different schools, just as children from affluent families do. (Of the 53 private schools registered in the voucher plan, 80 percent are sectarian. Of the sectarian schools, 90 percent are Catholic.) The court ruled against the voucher plan on two grounds: it violated the U.S. and state constitutions regarding the separation of church and state, and it violated the Ohio constitutional provision that requires that state laws have statewide application.

If one were to speak about the Cleveland Voucher Plan as an experiment, then one would have to say that as of May, 1997, the null hypothesis has been affirmed.

But politics is not like a scientific laboratory and the affirmation of a null hypothesis is often merely a place to pause while the combatants consider what new strategies to employ. Immediately after the Court of Appeals found the plan unconstitutional, David Brennan said that the state would attempt to fix the language of the law so as to overcome the objections. Constitutional issues aside, the State Senate Education Committee, which was already scheduled to hold hearings concerning the primary and secondary portions of the fiscal 1998–99 budget bill, began doing so. Opposition came from the Cleveland Teachers Union, the ACLU, People for the American Way, and a coalition of liberal religious and secular groups calling itself Citizens Against Vouchers. At one hearing, Ron Marec, president of the Ohio Federation of

Teachers, argued that when the cost of transportation, program administration and non-classroom services are added to the cost of tuition, each voucher increases by 90 percent — from $1,783 per pupil to $3,375. Noting that the state had hired a fleet of taxis to deliver students to participating voucher schools in Cleveland, he said that the transportation cost is $629 per pupil, which far exceeds the costs of transporting students to public schools.

The future of vouchers in Ohio remains an open question. In part, the answer depends on what the Ohio Supreme Court decides about the Court of Appeals decision. But it may also be affected by a change that is taking place in the relationship of local government to the Cleveland public schools. The current Mayor, Michael White, broke precedent in 1995 by lobbying for his own candidates for the school board and was successful in his efforts. The reform-minded school board, however, failed to make a dent in changing the direction of the school system. In 1996, he began seeking formal changes in the state law which would allow him to appoint the School Board and a chief executive officer to run the Cleveland School System. That proposed legislation provides that four years after the Mayor's Board takes control, voters will be allowed to decide whether to keep the schools under the mayor's control or not. It was supported by Governor Voinovich. Mayor White, in turn, supported the pilot voucher plan.

Part Two

Because the Cleveland Voucher Plan was limited to the City of Cleveland, and because there are very few Jews living within the city limits, there has been no direct impact of the plan on the Jewish community. The issue of vouchers, however, has been a topic of interest for Jews in Cleveland. While most of the discussion over vouchers has mirrored the discussion among the larger population, at least one talk about religion and education, delivered in the context of a zoning variance hearing, may be of interest to those concerned with the constitutional debate over vouchers.

As one might expect, there is a division of opinion on vouchers among Jews in Cleveland. But in truth, there is no debate. As with the division of opinion in the general public, opponents talk past each other. One side talks about the forest; the other about the trees. Opponents of vouchers express concern about their impact on the "system" of public education as an organic whole; proponents focus on individual students, or at least students from poor families.

When the voucher proposal was being debated in the budget bill, Jewish organizations like the American Jewish Committee in Cleveland began receiving fax messages from the state teachers union inviting us to join in publicly opposing it. The local Community Relations Council (CRC) held a meeting on April 12, 1995, to discuss the subject. The CRC voted unanimously to join a coalition of non-Jewish groups opposing the proposed program. The CRC was joined by the local chapters of the American Jewish Congress and the Anti-Defamation League.

The CRC supported their decision by arguing that vouchers would take the top students out of the public schools, leaving only the less talented and less motivated ones. Furthermore, vouchers would take needed money from the public schools. Neither change would "cure the ills of the Cleveland school system." Whether or not retaining the best students and the money were enough to solve those ills was not a question that was posed. The second argument in support of their opposition to vouchers was that the proposed program "appears to violate the Establishment Clause of the First Amendment of the United States Constitution." As far as the fact that vouchers meant the religious schools would receive taxpayer money through tuition payment, the CRC expressed a concern that the funds provided from vouchers could realistically be used to fund a school's religious curriculum. They asserted that "the (Supreme) Court has struck down nearly every form of financial aid to parochial schools at the elementary and secondary levels."

On the general topic of vouchers and choice, Jews opposing vouchers regularly adopt the position that the focal point must be on the health of the public schools; they bind together our diverse society. In response to the charge that all people should be given a choice of the schools to which they send their children, speakers argue that there should be resistance because the push for choice and vouchers has come from conservative think-tanks, Republicans, and conservative Christian groups, all of whom are more ideological, self-interested, concerned with deregulation and wedded to market place forces and competition. Behind all of these ideas, some people claim, is a desire to create homogenous environments, that is, to avoid Blacks.

Support for vouchers is more prevalent among those Jews supporting day schools. They argue that all children are entitled to a general secular education aided by the taxpayer and that this right should not be denied to children who attend non-public school. Some publicly stated that they hoped that students in their schools who are currently on scholarships might one day be eligible for vouchers. While they did not say so publicly, in conversations I had with them, a few indicated that they hoped that if vouchers were made available to less financially able Jewish families who are reluctant to accept "charity" and who feel compelled to send their children to public schools, that they may be more inclined to send those children to day schools.

Most of the proponents with whom I have talked argue that vouchers would lessen the pressure on the schools to do independent fund-raising from the Jewish community. The percentage of students on scholarships in the five day schools in Cleveland ranges from 20 to 35 percent. Generally, tuition covers only between 60–65 percent of the total costs borne by the schools. The rest is raised by each school's independent fund-raising efforts. However, they generally doubt that vouchers will affect Jewish day schools, since most of them are already filled to capacity. One day school principal expressed concern that the school could quickly get accustomed to the available money and then suddenly discover that it was no longer available, either as a result of a lawsuit or because of a change in the state legislature.[1]

Is the Jewish division merely a reflection of the more general set of arguments being made? While it appears that way, the issue of religions and education took on a somewhat different, albeit subtle coloration, during a hearing for a zoning variance before the Zoning Board of the city of Beachwood Ohio, a suburb of Cleveland.

Beachwood is a predominantly non-Orthodox Jewish suburb. For the past seven years, negotiations have been underway between the growing Orthodox Jewish population of Beachwood and the city's Zoning Board about the rezoning of land in the community that would permit the building of a campus of Orthodox Jewish institutions that includes two synagogues (Chabad and Young Israel of Beachwood), two mikvahs and a Jewish girl's high school (Yavnah) currently housed at the Hebrew Academy building in another Cleveland suburb.

The institution most in question for inclusion in the campus was the girls high school. At the hearing, Rabbi Sholom Strajcher, Education Director of the Hebrew Academy, argued that in Judaism prayer and religious study are closely aligned. Both take place within the synagogue and within the day school. Implicit in his argument was that from the perspective of Orthodox Judaism, education is entailed in the concept of the free exercise of religion.

What if this concept were to be applied to the question of vouchers? Is it possible that a different kind of debate could be generated that would pose a different set of questions? Is it possible that such a debate could be about whether vouchers ought to be interpreted in light of the Free Exercise Clause and not the Establishment Clause?

Perhaps there is some implicit recognition within the Jewish community that the traditional community relations view of the topic is in need of reconsideration. One may hope that in future discussions between Orthodox and non-Orthodox Jews, the question of vouchers might be discussed empirically and not ideologically.

Endnotes

1. State funds currently being paid to religious schools pay for materials for the study of the hard sciences, mathematics textbooks, computer equipment, transportation to and from the school, and in some cases for school breakfasts and lunches. Monies for auxiliary services include speech and hearing therapists, reimbursements for secretarial assistance to fulfill government regulations. The Ohio Department of Education's Non-Public Administrative Cost Reimbursement Report reveals that the state reimbursements to all parochial schools in Ohio for non-adminstrative procedures amounts to well over $60 million. Of that total, over $750,000 are given to twelve Jewish day schools in the state. Of that sum, four-fifths are given to day schools in Cleveland.

School Choice: What Does the Evidence Say?

Jay P. Greene

There is no shortage of theories about the effects of school choice, but there is a shortage of evidence. We have heard a good deal about some of these theories from our other speakers. Some suggest that school choice should improve education because competition helps improve the quality of any product or service. Some suggest that school choice is beneficial because it cultivates a stronger commitment to education on the part of parents. The act of choosing alone gives parents a stake in schools and helps improve the outcomes. Some suggest that school choice is desirable because it more efficiently matches student needs and school abilities. Children learn best in many different ways. Choice allows parents to find the schools that offer what is best for their children rather than being stuck in a one-size-fits-none public system.

But there are also a series of plausible theories, some of which have been offered by other speakers, that suggest that school choice might not be beneficial. Some worry that markets in education do not operate like markets for other goods and services. Perhaps many parents are poorly informed about what constitutes a suitable education for their children. Perhaps many parents are disinterested in their children's education. Without widespread quality information and widespread interest by parents, choice may allow access to desirable schools for some, while impoverishing the experience of the rest. Some worry that school choice will undermine the integration, tolerance, and commitment to public spiritedness that we hope children learn in schools. Some worry about the constitutionality of school choice plans that include religious schools.

As you can see, there are many reasonable-sounding theories for and against school choice. What is lacking in most discussions of the subject is evidence on the actual effects of school choice programs. This inattention to evidence is somewhat understandable because we have relatively little experience with school choice. Of the thousands of school districts around the country, only two have adopted publicly funded school choice programs: Milwaukee and, more recently, Cleveland. I will present what we have learned from these two programs about the academic effects of school choice. I will also discuss some of the evidence on questions of integration, tolerance, and public spiritedness in public and private schools. While the amount of evidence on school choice is limited, what we do know is very encouraging about the benefits of choice. It is certainly encouraging enough to suggest that additional pilot programs should be initiated and carefully studied.

The Evidence from Milwaukee

The first publicly funded school choice program was adopted in Milwaukee. It is hardly an ideal test of the school choice concept. A very small number of students were allowed to participate. All students had to be low-income and most were minority students with a host of educational disadvantages. Students could only choose among a handful of secular, private schools, which excluded almost 90 percent of the private school spaces in Milwaukee, including some of the most established and respected schools. And schools were paid only the state contribution to the per capita cost of educating students in the Milwaukee public schools (MPS), which is about half of the per capita expenditures in MPS.

But the Milwaukee school choice program had one very nice feature: it required that students be admitted by lottery to the private schools when spaces were over-subscribed. This lottery created randomly assigned treatment and control groups, like in a medical experiment, where the two groups are initially identical. Any differences between the academic achievement of those accepted at random to the choice program and those rejected at random can reasonably be attributed to the effect of the program itself.

Harvard researchers Paul Peterson, Jiangtao Du and I examined the results of this randomized experiment. We found that after four years in the private schools, the choice students outperformed the control group on standardized math tests by 11 points. Choice students outpaced the control group in MPS on standardized reading tests by 6 points after four years. These gains are moderately large and statistically significant. To put the gains in perspective, the math improvement is equivalent to about one-half of the difference between white and minority test scores nationwide. The reading gain is equivalent to more than one-fourth of the average gap separating white and minority test scores.

These findings differed from the evaluation produced by a team selected by the state superintendent of education, who had sued to stop the choice program. That evaluation found no meaningful effects of school choice on academic performance but did find considerable enthusiasm for the program from parents. Taken at its word, this state-selected evaluation says that school choice does not hurt or help test scores, but does make parents very happy, all for about half of the cost of a public education. But the failure of the state-selected evaluation to focus on the randomized experiment prevented them from obtaining a clear picture of the program's effects. Princeton economist Cecelia Rouse independently examined the data, focusing on the randomized experiment, and essentially found the same results that we had. While the Milwaukee choice program has its limitations and while the evidence it produced is hampered by missing information, the results suggest important benefits of school choice that should be examined more closely in new programs that can more carefully be studied.

The Evidence from Cleveland

The second publicly funded school choice program started last year in Cleveland. This program is also interesting because it is the first to offer the choice of a religious as well as secular education. With Paul Peterson at Harvard and William Howell at Stanford, I have looked at the satisfaction of parents with the program so far. We found that the parents of students in the choice program are significantly more satisfied with various aspects of their child's education than the parents of students who were offered a scholarship but chose to return to the Cleveland public schools. The choice parents were almost twice as likely to be very satisfied with the quality of teaching, school safety, and nearly three times as likely to be very satisfied with the teaching of moral values.

We also found that a number of concerns about school choice were not manifesting themselves in the Cleveland program. We found that the most important consideration in parents' choices was academic quality, not location, sports or religion, as some had feared. We found no evidence that private schools were "creaming" applicants by selecting wealthier or more advantaged students.

We have also had access to the test scores of students at the two largest private schools participating in the choice program. Hope Central and Hope Academy, two campuses of a newly formed, secular organization, consist entirely of choice students and contain almost one-fourth of the students in the choice program who had previously attended public schools. Students at these schools have shown significant improvement between the standardized test results taken from when they entered and the results from the end of their first year.

While these parental satisfaction and test score results are encouraging about the benefits of the program, it should be noted that the high quality random assignment research design used in Milwaukee is not possible in Cleveland. Also, educational programs usually take a few years for their effects to become clear. We may not have greater confidence in any conclusions about the Cleveland program's consequences for another year or two.

The Evidence on Integration, Tolerance, and Public Spiritedness

We do not yet have any direct information about the effects of school choice on the civic values of students. I have, however, examined data on the integration and democratic values found in public and private schools from which we might extrapolate to the expanded access to private education that choice would allow. According to the evidence I have found in the National Education Longitudinal Study (NELS) sponsored by the Department of Education, private schools are actually better integrated racially, report a greater degree of racial tolerance, and display a higher amount of commitment to helping the community.

These surprising results suggest that public schools may not be what we imagine or hope they are. Attendance at a public school is usually based on where students live, yet housing can be highly racially segregated. This reliance on attendance zones undermines the "common school" ideal that we have for education. Additional research is necessary to identify why there are higher levels of racial tolerance and public-spiritedness in private schools. But the evidence from NELS suggests that our long-held assumption that government operation of schools is essential for ensuring the proper education of future generations of citizens may be faulty.

What Does the Evidence Mean for Jews and School Choice?

The long-standing support that Jews have expressed for public education is, I think, really support for the purposes of that education. If we learn that academic achievement, integration, and civic values can be promoted more effectively by school choice than by the use of public funds only at government operated schools, then I think our support should and will shift. Jews are similarly committed to the goal of universal access to quality health care but have shied away from government operation of the health care system because it is feared that this would undermine the desired goal.

Constitutional questions about school choice including religious schools also concern many Jews. Here again I think the issue hinges on what the evidence shows to be effective, not on inconsistent application of Constitutional law. The odd truth is that Jews overwhelmingly support school choice in higher education and in pre-school. We like the fact that the government offers Pell Grants and subsidized loans for students to use at any college or university of their choice, public or private, religious or secular. A Pell Grant can be used at Yeshiva University, Brigham Young, or Baylor if a student wishes. Similarly, the day care tax credit, which is to be expanded in President Clinton's most recent budget, is essentially a voucher good for an education at any pre-school, public or private, religious or secular. The only places where we do not have school choice that includes religious education are in kindergarten through twelfth grade. The use of public funds for school choice, whether pre-school, high school, or college, is not a government establishment of religion, but government support of an effective education that people choose.

The central issue is whether there is sufficient evidence to embrace school choice programs. The initial evidence is encouraging for choice. We need a series of new, publicly funded programs with a high quality random-assignment research design to draw more definitive conclusions. I believe that Jews concerned about the quality of education should support additional experiments and be willing to expand or abandon the programs based on the results over several years.

ROMAN CATHOLIC PERSPECTIVES

James T. McHugh

I am pleased to take part in this symposium with scholars and interested persons from the Jewish community to consider the matter of school vouchers. I will briefly comment on the value of vouchers for society and for public schools, but I will focus more on a Catholic perspective on vouchers. In order to have someone express the interest of the Catholic Church and Catholic schools, you could have invited any Bishop in the United States. Any one of us would have said the same thing. We all have the same interest—we are unequivocally supportive of a voucher system that will benefit parents, children, and all schools, but will include (in the "all schools") Catholic schools as well. In my own state, New Jersey, we have pursued the adoption of a voucher bill very strongly over the past four years, although it doesn't seem to make much progress. And now, with the crisis in New Jersey in terms of public education, I wonder what will happen to it. As I left this morning to come here, the papers were again filled with the news of the New Jersey Supreme Court's rejection of the funding mechanism for public education, even though it's supportive of the standards proposed by Governor Whitman. In any case, my purpose this afternoon is to try to emphasize the fact that vouchers are of value to parents and children, they are of value to society, and they are of value to church-sponsored schools.

First of all, what they do for parents and children is enable choice. In fact, vouchers are only a subdivision of the whole concept of school choice. They provide children who receive them an incentive to excel, and they give parents a greater sense of involvement and control in the schools their children attend. According to public opinion surveys, there is increasing interest in and support for voucher programs across the United States, and that includes voucher programs that would involve or include church-related schools. They benefit society in providing an alternative to public education, not as an antagonistic system, but as a cooperating one.

There's no question that the role of Catholic schools is a major part of the discussion because among church-related or church-sponsored schools, Catholic schools probably are, numerically, in the majority among other religious denominations. Catholic schools bring to the whole educational mix a number of advantages in the United States. I might emphasize that Catholic schools today are largely middle-income and lower-income schools. There were some references this morning to the Catholic schools, and especially, *urban* Catholic schools. The history of the Catholic population in the United States has been a history of urban location, so in any of our big cities you will find those huge churches, and usually schools, convents, rectories—all that goes with the so-called "parish plant." The original Catholic population, of course, has shifted now to the suburbs. We find an increasing suburban development with new parishes, new schools, rectories, and all the rest. But we still have those large parish plants in the cities. And those inner city parishes are now very much a mixed population—a mixed population racially, ethnically, and religiously. Nonetheless, Catholic schools in many cases remain open and vibrant in the cities.

We consider Catholic schools a benefit to the country. They constitute an educational presence that brings academic competence, a sense of religious values, and a history of service. There are numerous studies that demonstrate the educational competence of the Catholic schools—Coleman's research, endorsed by Chubb and Moe, for example, and many other studies too numerous to mention. In New Jersey, the key words of the Governor's program for public education cited by the N.J. Supreme Court was that "the schools were to provide thorough and efficient education." I submit that the Catholic schools measure up to that not only in New Jersey, but throughout the country.

The second characteristic or quality of Catholic schools is they are a system of schools committed to religious faith and values, and the religious faith and values are integrated into the whole of the school's existence. However, the religious faith and values do not dominate the curriculum. They do not undermine the teaching of the sciences, or history or languages or math. The religious faith and values are not secret, mysterious, or in any way overly compelling. The whole sense of the religious spirit of the school is not for proselytizing, nor for separatism, but rather, as a beneficial influence to all of the students—even those who, from time to time, not being Catholic, may wish to absent themselves. The religious component is integrated with societal values, and the schools include all the other characteristics of American schools or American communities—Boy Scouts and Girl Scouts, competitive sports, involvement in public service and public ventures.

Thirdly, Catholic schools through the years have provided service to the Catholic community and to the overall community as well. Traditionally, Catholic schools have serviced the poor, the disadvantaged, and the various generations of immigrants as they came to our country. I can speak more personally about the service dimension of the schools because, as I said before, while our schools are now largely suburban, there is also a major component of urban schools. In the city of Camden we have six grade schools with approximately 1,200 to 1,500 students. Probably there could be more if there was an opportunity for parents to pay the tuition that is an absolute necessity in the Catholic schools. In addition to the support that comes from tuition, the diocese subsidizes these six schools to the amount of about $1 million a year. The Catholic enrollment in the schools varies. In one school, it is no more than 5 percent, in another school it is about 30 percent, and in the other four it is somewhere between 75 percent and 85 percent. The Catholic schools that exist throughout the country are not going out of business; they are very much here to stay. But anytime there is discussion of vouchers, the religious nature of the schools always comes up as a stumbling block. But I think we've had a very good discussion this morning about the constitutional issues.

Nonetheless, Paul Peterson of Harvard makes the case quite well that "when religious issues are set aside and vouchers are evaluated in educational terms, the findings are clear. Vouchers work for the inner city poor. Low-income families receiving vouchers are pleased with their children's schools even when the grants amount to less than half of what the public spends. Voucher students are more apt to stay in school, learn more, and earn their high school diplomas. No wonder inner-city residents, when asked, strongly support school choice." As Catholics, we think of our schools in the context of religious pluralism, which is usually referred to as one of the great benefits of our country. It sort of follows through on those constitutional guarantees of freedom of religion, although I sometimes wonder if we have freedom of religion in the United States anymore. I think it's been switched somewhat to freedom from religion. In any case, in our tests for pluralism, we expect that involvement in the pluralistic mix of the country means that all religious communities are included in this society in national affairs without having to compromise their religious identity. And secondly, pluralism doesn't mean, ultimately, secularism. In the context then of pluralism, the Catholic schools exist and survive. So we do not look on vouchers as a survival mechanism, but more as a matter of justice. Over the past five years Catholic schools throughout the United States have begun an upswing. We went from a high point, probably in the 50s, to a lower point in the 70s, and now we have begun to see the enrollment increase again. We've lost a number of schools, but from what we have seen, the situation now seems to be stable right across the country.

So we are not depending on a voucher system as a survival mechanism for Catholic schools. We will probably continue to grow, even without vouchers, at a very measured pace. Vouchers will not create a massive influx of funds. But they will help parents meet tuition costs. Nor will vouchers create an explosion or a massive expansion of Catholic schools, partially because many of our people have moved to the suburbs, and they are satisfied with their suburban schools. In fact, some of them have chosen the place of their homes by reason of their confidence in the schools of a particular community. However, vouchers will allow choice, and they will result in some moderate expansion and some upgrading of our facilities.

Nonetheless, fear of Catholic schools persists in our society, and it is stirred by every discussion of a voucher program. The experience of Catholic educa*tion is one to which the Catholic church is committed. Vouchers would be helpful, but are not indispensable. We believe in vouchers as a matter of justice. Catholic parents and non-Catholic parents who choose, in increasing numbers, to send their children to Catholic schools should not be prevented from doing so simply by reason of the cost. And to the degree that a voucher system is an equalizing system, it can be a great benefit to parents and children and to the schools themselves. But it will not make an overwhelming difference to the Catholic church, which will survive and continue its mission, or fail to do so, for other reasons.

A Minority Perspective

Floyd Flake

This discussion about the direction and future of American education is one of the most important debates taking place in America today. I am most concerned about the individuals and populations who have been left out of the system. I am concerned about what it means for American society, and what it means for the many young people who have been left behind in communities where public education is not meeting their needs. I support vouchers because I dare to believe that they represent perhaps our last hope for a quality education for many of the young people of this country.

Years ago, in the early 1970s, when I served as an Associate Dean at Lincoln University in Pennsylvania, and then as Dean of Students and Dean of the Chapel at Boston University, I realized that many young people were coming to college out of the inner cities without the skills to compete in their new environment. In too many instances they either did not have the tools they needed to stay until graduation; or if they did graduate, they would not necessarily have what is needed to function in society.

In 1976, when I was asked to come and pastor a church in Jamaica Queens, I decided that one of the first things I would do was introduce education to young people at a much earlier stage in their development. We decided to build our own school in this one parish, but we discovered during its construction that we did not know for certain how many young people would appear on the first day. We anticipated about 75 children. Instead, we had 234. This was done without any testing or selection process.

What we discovered was that young people who are in a disciplined learning environment can indeed be educated to their potential, provided only that their teachers' primary focus was education and not politics. I mean that teachers need to be primarily concerned about the education of children, rather than about their own seniority or their ranking in the competitive profile among other teachers around the city. We have discovered over these last fourteen years that you can take even a seemingly troubled student out of the public system, put him into a private or a parochial system, and he or she will demonstrate the capability and the potential to achieve. I am not arguing for the elimination of public education. I am insisting that it had better do what it was intended to do, which is to produce young people capable of functioning in any environment they find themselves, and who are not held back or held down because the institutions from which they graduated did not properly prepare them.

I started my career as a social worker with a Head Start program in Dayton, Ohio. I found it most interesting that when we tested children who were graduating from Head Start, they scored at the second grade level. When we went back a few years later and tested the same children, the majority of them were still at the second grade level because the institutions could not cope with students who had an accelerated pace. Rather than trying to move the other school children to the level of those accelerated students, they took the accelerated students, dropped them into the bunch, and then brought all of the students back down to the level of the lowest common denominator. That is not what I think an educational system ought to do.

I come from Houston, Texas, where in the early stages of my life I rode a bus past three white schools to get to a Black school out in the country. There were four teachers who taught eight grades, so open classrooms were not a new idea for me when, in the early 70s, people began to talk about them as if it they were innovative. Now those four teachers demonstrated, by virtue of their concern and commitment for students, a kind of in loco parentis attitude that said, "Every child here belongs to me, and I will educate this child as if he were my own because I want to give him the very best." They made us expunge words like "can't" from our vocabulary; they challenged us to understand that despite the fact that our books had already been used by students in white schools, and there was no place for us to put our names on the inner cover, that did not matter. What did matter was that we got information from those books and were prepared so competently that our color would not be a barrier for us when we grew up and had to compete in the larger society.

Interestingly enough, when integration and bussing were pushed in the late sixties and early seventies, people thought that at last this was the panacea—this was it. This was the utopian concept of education. If we could but integrate African-American youth with youth of other cultures and other ethnic backgrounds, then at last we would have solved the problem of education in America. What happened, though, was that too often the buses went only one way. I was in Boston at the time of the integration of the schools in south Boston, when Judge Garrity had to be appointed the trustee over the school system. Many schools where African-American teachers had been serving as effective role models for their students were now turned into vocational schools or, in some instances, shut down altogether. The white children who should have been coming to those schools in those communities were not coming.

The "cream-of-the crop" in almost any community can get into schools where they will get a proper education. But that ignores all those young people who will never be able to get a proper education in the schools they are compelled to attend. It's also the case that many programs for the gifted include few among their student population who are of African-American or Latino descent. Conversely, African-American and Latino students make up the largest population in special education classes.

There has been unfairness in the system, and until we can deal with this unfairness I believe that we have to offer as many alternatives as possible, not only to ensure the maintenance of public education, but to make public education as competitive as possible. I believe that charter schools and vouchers are ways to make public education responsive, as it would be if it did not hold a monopoly on every young person obliged to stay within its system. I assert, as vehemently as I possibly can, that vouchers make good sense. Vouchers mean that a number of young people, even though only a limited few, will be able at last to escape a system that does not provide them a competitive education.

When we introduced our scholarship program in New York, where I am a member of the committee, we received twenty thousand applicants for a school lottery that had only thirteen hundred places! That means there is real interest on the part of many people in these communities in finding some alternative to public school. My church provides a school for pre-K through 8th grade, for 480 students. We usually have 150 children on our waiting list. We've discovered that by offering these young people a second language (starting as early as three years old), most of them learn to speak Spanish to some degree. When they graduate from our school most of them go into Catholic high schools in New York because there are no African-American high schools for them. We really serve as a feeder school for the parochial school system, and the Catholic schools come to seek out our students. They do so because, first, our students can pass the test; second, they have been immersed in a disciplined learning environment; and third, they generally have the competence and capability to compete with the other students in that system. We have a graduation rate of 99 percent, and of that 99 percent who graduate from high school, 97 percent have gone on to college and graduated.

There are complex forces at work in the school question. The unions are coming from one direction, the teachers and educators from the other direction. They argue that a system of vouchers means the destruction of public education. Several years ago, when the automobile industry thought it had a complete monopoly, the "Big Three" manufacturers were putting out cars that we knew would be antiquated within three years. But when the Japanese came into our market and began to take market share away from the Big Three, these American companies decided it was time to produce a better product. The same thing happened at the U.S. Postal Service. While it was a monopoly standing alone it did not have to be responsive to the demands of its customers. But when Federal Express and UPS became more competitive, the postal system awakened to the reality that it was losing market share. I would argue that there are too many dollars available to the public school system today, too many dollars available to the union members for them to just sit back, watch themselves lose market share, and not try to create a better product. I think this is really the American way. We see it everywhere. If it is appropriate for automobiles, if it is appropriate for the U.S. Postal Service, then surely it ought to be appropriate for improving the education of our young people. We must create some competitiveness in the system or otherwise we will continue to throw our money down the drain and not get the kind of product that is needed.

I educate a child at Allen Christian School for $3,200 a year. The public system in the same community spends between $6,200 and $8,000 per child. I asked them to give me that money and give me an empty building. Give me no teachers, give me no sextons, no janitors, nothing. Just give me that empty building and those students and five years, and I can turn that school around. We need to create the alternatives. But I think the reason people react so vehemently against alternatives is that they really just don't want competition that might succeed.

I support competition, and I support vouchers. I believe they are important and they make good sense. Those who argue against them on constitutional grounds must also know that we have an obligation to educate all of our young people. And we already have the equivalent of a voucher system in place at the college level which no one considers unconstitutional. Students who receive Pell Grants are able to take them to a Notre Dame or a St. John's University to continue their education.

How are we going to get these inner city children to the position where they are competitive enough to participate and succeed in secondary and college education? Now we are saying that we are willing to help them at the upper end, if they survive until they get to college, but we're not ready to prepare students at the lower end to make it possible for more of them to get into those colleges and universities.

Another argument against vouchers is that giving a voucher does not mean that a student will really be able to go to a private school because he still won't have enough money to afford it. I see things from a different vantage point. Each time payments are due at Allen Christian School, I watch the grandparents, the uncles, the cousins, the friends of the family—whoever is willing to invest in that child—coming together to write the check to show their interest in the education of that child. I believe that somehow they will do it. I read one of the most profound stories in the *New York Daily News*, where a father said "I got one of the vouchers and I'm happy about it!" And they asked him how he was going to pay the balance if his child went to the school he had been admitted to. He said, "The balance is about eighteen hundred dollars. I will pay it, even if I have to get a second job. I'm prepared to do whatever I have to do to make an investment in my child."

Vouchers may not be the whole answer, but they are a good beginning, and we must all work together to make sure that those who represent special interests in this country and who oppose vouchers do not destroy a program that, I am convinced, offers great opportunities for the future of America.

THE EFFECT UPON PUBLIC SCHOOLS: FINANCING AND SUPPORT

Chester E. Finn, Jr.

I am humbled to be the only non-clergyman on this panel, participating with Bishop McHugh and the Congressman, Rev. Floyd Flake, in an exercise of extraordinary pluralistic planning. I'm going to start by saying that I have disagreed strongly with the stance of a significant swath of organized American Jewry regarding the topic of today's program. It seems to me that most American Jews have worked, conscientiously and quite effectively, to exercise educational choice for themselves and their children. They find a house near a public school that works well for their kids. They patronize private schools. They make it work. And yet, an extraordinary array of American-Jewish organizations seems hostile to the proposition that other people ought to be able to exercise those kinds of choices, too. A lot of organized American Jewry has bought into what I would call an "image" or "theory" of public education, and has overlooked much of the reality of American public education which Congressman Flake was describing. I think we must go back to basic questions as a starting point. Let me set three questions before you and then let us discuss how we might answer them today as opposed to how they might have been answered previously. Many organizations develop positions into which they eventually become frozen. Perhaps the old questions need new answers.

First, what is a public school? Second, for whose benefit do we operate public schools? Third, in a democracy, what are our rights with respect to schooling? Let us examine how the answers to these questions have evolved over the last thirty years since L.B.J. occupied the White House. Thirty years ago there were fairly clear answers to these questions that were taken for granted by most people. But they are far less clear today.

What is a public school? Thirty years ago we took for granted that a public school meant a school run by the government, a mostly uniform appendage of a state bureaucracy staffed by government employees, run according to government regulations, overseen by government administrators. Many people today are saying that a public school is any school that is open to the public, financed by the public, and accountable to public authorities for its performance, even if it is not run by the government directly. It may be run by a team of teachers, or a group of parents, or a community organization, a for-profit firm, perhaps even a church. It can be very different from the school situated a mile away. It is not necessarily staffed by government employees. Certainly it is not answerable for its procedures and actions to government bureaucrats.

Second question: For whose benefit do we have public schools? Thirty years ago there was a debate among economists about the relative portions of educational gains that should be classed as private benefit vs. public benefit. But we rarely doubted that the public schools existed for the benefit of "the public," of "society," or of "children and parents and taxpayers." How many people really believe that is the way things operate today? Today, I submit, we have many reasons to doubt that the public schools any longer operate day-to-day for the explicit and primary benefit of their customers. Indeed, on the contrary, in their day-to-day workings, budget decisions and policy priorities, many schools and school systems appear to be run for the benefit and convenience of their employees—their staffs and managers.

Third question: What are people's rights regarding schooling in a democracy? Thirty years ago we were preoccupied with giving everybody the right to attend school and not be barred by their color, disabilities or other characteristics. These were primarily group rights of access for once-victimized populations, and we did not pay much attention to individual or parent rights with respect to schooling. We also tended to trust the state to be just and fair and to look after our interests. If the state wanted to tell people which school to attend, or to move students from one school to another, we may have grumbled but we took for granted that the government knew best and was looking after our interest and the public interest. We had probably forgotten the admonition of John Stewart Mill, the great civil libertarian, who wrote about 140 years ago that "the state should leave to parents to obtain the education of their children where and how they please, and content itself with helping to pay the school fees. If this were done, there would be an end to the difficulties about what the state should teach, and how it should teach, which now convert the subject into a battleground for sects and parties."

He had it figured out, but we just forgot it. Today, though we have come to see schooling as a different sort of civil rights issue, as a matter better trusted to individuals and families than to the tender mercies of bureaucrats, politicians, judges and experts. Those battles among "sects and parties" have worn us down. The stranglehold that self-interested "stakeholder" groups within the education field have gained over policy decisions bearing on public schooling has left millions of people doubting that the state is really looking after anybody's interests any longer. Particularly in our minority communities, as we have heard twice today in eloquent testimony, we see that state-run education often fails to meet the most fundamental expectations of parents. They should be confident that their children will spend their days in a safe place where they will be looked after by people who care for them and who teach them to read and write and count. Is that too much to expect of a school? Yet one cannot take it for granted anymore that this is what is happening in the school that the state insists your child attend. That is why 27,000 people sought to avail themselves of 1,300 opportunities to escape New York City public schools in favor of private schools. Who are these people? They are not the economically secure on Park Avenue who already have exercised school choice. To be eligible, they had to be poor.

In these 30 years, we have also become more aware of the oddness of this one public policy domain being about the only place where the normal rules and rights of a democracy don't apply. We can live where we choose, even if we are on welfare. We can eat what we like, even if we are on food stamps. We can go to the doctor that we favor, even if we are on Medicaid. We can attend the college of our choice, even if we pay for it with Pell Grants or other scholarships. We can travel where we like, even if we get there by public transportation. In the midst of all that, elementary and secondary education is a sort of policy ghetto. It is just about the only place where we take for granted that involuntary, government-run, no-choice state monopoly, state regulation and control should rule our lives, and this in respect to something so very crucial to our lives. If the state were doing a really good job, people might be a little less cranky, but it is not doing a good job.

In response to the third question I put before you, then, we no longer assume that the state is the primary protector of our rights with respect to education. We are much more inclined to want to exercise those rights for ourselves, as individuals and as families. In the last thirty years, we have begun to lose faith in large bureaucratic monopolies of every kind. You won't find a private sector organization any longer that runs as a large bureaucratic monopoly with top-down controls, vast middle-management, uniform controls over the means of production and the inputs. Every effective private organization today says to its line managers, "We're going to let you organize your operation as you see fit, but we are going to hold you accountable for your results." This notion, which has proven effective in the private sector and corresponds to every sane management theory that I have seen, is now even beginning to percolate slowly in government. It is usually called "reinventing government." It gives rise to the notion that governments should steer rather than row, that government should outsource some of its activities. That is just beginning to make its way into elementary and secondary education. One manifestation of it is called "charter schools," now numbering about five hundred schools in twenty-six states, and soon to be seven or eight hundred schools. This is larger even than the voucher movement today. Charters and vouchers together are the most visible manifestation of the movement in the K–12 education to reinvent government. They indicate that education, too, doesn't have to be run by the government to be a public good.

Let me say a bit more regarding vouchers. There are privately-funded versions, by my count, in thirty-two cities today. The New York City program, funded by private philanthropists, is the most recent of them. In every one of those cities, the demand exceeds the supply. There are people lined up for the lottery. There is no constitutional issue because only private dollars are involved. The problem is that private dollars, even in our generous country, are never going to produce a full-scale program for the massive numbers of students. That is why the publicly funded variety is important. They don't have to be called vouchers. In some places they are called scholarships. They are different approaches to the same end. Meanwhile, as you know, there are already two publicly-funded voucher programs up and running today, in Milwaukee and Cleveland. There are also a few left-over arrangements in little towns in Vermont and Maine that are vouchers in all but name.

What do we know about this phenomenon? First, we know that demand exceeds supply and that there is beginning to be some supply-side response. Vouchers tend to cause people to create new schools like Congressman Flake's. Schools are cropping up in Cleveland and Milwaukee today. There is clear research evidence, especially from Milwaukee, with four years of data, that the children in situations with vouchers are learning more than those without them. We know that both parents and children like them. What about popular support more broadly conceived? I am not sure about the effects of vouchers, but I can relate something interesting about charter schools, because we at the Hudson Institute have been working on a study of such schools for the past two years. Twenty percent of children attending American charter schools were not attending public schools previously. They were home schooled, or they were drop-outs, or they were attending private schools. There is an interesting new competition developing between charter schools and private schools in some communities, and that is a very important development to consider. I think it is fair to say that twenty percent of the students in charter schools would not be in any form of public school if they were not exercising school choice and attending charter schools. That widens the net of public education and enlarges the population served by public schools. I would also dare say that it is broadening the support base for public education—but not the old bureaucratic monopoly version.

I am not here to sell you vouchers, I am here to encourage your support of school choice and the marvelous variety of forms that it now takes. I am here to caution you about the intense resistance that this movement is encountering—resistance to choice in general and vouchers in particular. Some of it comes from private schools that either have a cushy arrangement with their tuition payers or are genuinely worried about the government regulation that they fear will come with vouchers. This is not an insignificant consideration, especially when we look at what has happened in private colleges over the years. But most opposition comes from defenders of the public school status quo. They want to protect the public school monopoly and prevent or limit these schemes of choices from really developing. To my mind, though, it is no longer a question in America whether we will have school choice. We have it now, and it is spreading. It is only a question of how fast, in which forms, and where next? An abstract, theoretical question was asked: Would vouchers be a good thing? Well, we have them now, and the question today is not whether, but where next, and how many, and under which rules, and with which constitutional overlays? The genie is out of the bottle and it is not going back in! I think this is going to keep happening and it makes me glad. I am glad when I read about 27,000 kids wanting 1,300 openings. That says to me there is a need in this society that has to be met, and school choice is going to be one of the ways of meeting it. I am glad when I can be here with people like Bishop McHugh and Congressman Flake, and I'm actually redoubled in my enthusiasm when I see who is lined up against school choice. Once in a while, you figure out what you are for by looking at who is against it. Look at who is against school choice and decide if you are not for it even more strongly than you were yesterday.

SECTION TWO:

SCHOOL VOUCHER PROGRAMS AND TRADITIONAL PRINCIPLES OF CHURCH-STATE SEPARATION

INTRODUCTION

Marshall J. Breger

Many in the Jewish community (in particular the defense organizations such as American Jewish Congress, American Jewish Committee and the Anti-Defamation League) feel there is no need to consider the policy issues surrounding school choice and school vouchers, since the entire project fails the threshold test of constitutionality. In this section, we will consider school voucher programs in light of traditional principles of the separation of church and state.

This section includes an introduction to the law of church and state relations by Professor Robert Destro, co-author of the standard law school casebook in the field, *Religious Liberty in a Pluralistic Society*. It is followed by a roundtable on church-state issues drawn from the May 1997 conference on school vouchers and the Jewish community which serves as the basis for this volume.

Since the conference, the courts have handed down two decisions that particularly bear on this area. On June 23, 1997, the Supreme Court decided *Agostini v. Felton*, which found that a federally funded program providing supplemental, remedial instruction to disadvantaged children on a neutral basis is not invalid under the Establishment Clause when such instruction is given by government employees on the premise of sectarian schools.

And in June 1998 the Wisconsin Supreme Court in *Jackson v. Benson* found constitutional the Milwaukee voucher scheme discussed in our first section. While it is likely that the case will be appealed to the United States Supreme Court, this decision means that—unless the Court stays the program pending its review—the Milwaukee experiment will be in full force this fall and the programs can be reviewed on policy grounds.

To help us read the tea leaves, we have asked six eminent scholars of church-state law, coming from a variety of perspectives, to add their views on the meaning of *Agostini* for the voucher debate. Together with our roundtable participants, this group helps us understand the unfolding legal debate over the constitutionality of school vouchers.

The contributors to this section try to move the discussion one step beyond past decisions, to talk about how the law might well look in the future. There are many questions to ask: Are vouchers a "neutral" activity? Does the likely positive impact on parochial schools create the danger of "excessive entanglement?" How much does the intent of the government authority creating a voucher system matter? In particular, we will consider whether a school voucher program could be structured without violating traditional principles of church-state separation, or whether we should consider changing traditional doctrine if it is not consonant with voucher schemes.

In short, we try to talk about both theory and practice, and to work out what the limits of government assistance in this area might be.

The History of the "Wall of Separation": Church and State in Constitutional Tradition

Robert Destro

In the United States, the law permits universal access to society's opportunities, benefits, and social obligations without regard to religious faith. In practice, however, it was (and remains) inevitable that social and political structures reflecting the perspective of the dominant religious faiths would (and will) cause problems for religious minorities.

The experience of religious minorities in the public (or "common") schools is well-documented in the state and federal case law. From its inception in the 1830s through 1860, the Common School Movement had several basic goals: 1) to provide schooling for all white children, either partially or wholly at public expense; 2) to encourage or require school attendance; 3) to foster the moral, political, and economic improvement of the citizenry (especially those of the "lower classes") through a program of civics and "non-sectarian" religious instruction; 4) to create training programs for teachers; and 5) to establish some measure of state control over all of these processes.

The educational and political strategies collectively known as "school choice" are controversial because the advocates for common schooling have been so successful, both in achieving the broad outlines of their political and social agendas, and in assimilating religious and many minorities into the mainstream of American life and culture. As early as 1880, a writer in *Scribner's Monthly* observed that: "We have made a sort of God of our common school system. It is treason to speak a word against it."

Today's debates over school choice are often couched in incendiary language. Though we have expanded our concern to include all children, regardless of race, the issues and goals facing the community are very much the same in the 1990s as they were in the 1830s.

What is "Choice" in Education?

I begin with a simple, yet often unstated, fact: from the perspective of the consumers of educational services—that is, parents, children, and taxpayers, primary and secondary education in the United States is not a matter of "choice." It is compulsory. Every state requires children to attend school, and will prosecute parents who refuse or neglect to educate them. Most states prescribe minimum standards for educational content, facilities, and teachers, and will enforce them vigorously. There is growing political and professional support for early childhood education, and calls for minimum educational and facility standards for day care centers are heard with increasing frequency. The inevitable next step will be to debate whether to make both mandatory. Education programs concerning human sexuality, drug and alcohol abuse, AIDS prevention, the use and distribution of contraceptives, and a whole host of programs on other sensitive topics (most recently, "multi-culturalism") inexorably metamorphose from "experimental, pilot programs" to required courses.

On a more tangible level, intense political and judicial battles are fought regularly over mandatory student assignment plans, school funding levels, and the administration of "magnet" school programs. It matters little whether the issue is busing for school desegregation, a redrawing of district lines to reflect demographic change and diversity, or the availability (or lack thereof) of education for children with special needs: choice in education, or, more appropriately, lack of choice, is a perennial and sensitive issue. It has been for a long time.

Last, but certainly not least, is the question of money. The cost of public education is borne by all the taxpayers, who have no more "choice" in the matter of making timely tax payments than the "choice" they will have in the face of death. Public education is big business, but with one important difference: it has no publicly-funded competition. Neither taxpayers nor consumers can vote with their wallets; they pay for the service whether it meets their needs or not. Choice is "extra." According to the 1990 *Statistical Abstract of the United States,* federal, state and local government support for public education totaled $148.6 billion in 1986, an average of $3733.67 for each child enrolled in the public schools. Private sector spending on non-public education during the same period amounted to $13.2 billion, an average of $2421.13 per child.

Because education funding is the largest single item in the budget of most local governments, and the school system may often be one of the largest employers in a community, issues which affect either education funding or policy become political issues of the first order as their effect ripples through the affected sectors of the electorate. As political issues, issues of education policy are subject to all of the factional cross-pressures, log-rolling and legal disputes which affect other aspects of the political process. From the perspective of those who provide and control public education, the range of permissible choice among legitimate alternatives is usually limited only by the amount of money available, and what the political traffic will bear.

Toss the possibility of parental choice into this roiling cauldron of hot political and social issues, and the mixture becomes volatile indeed. Fund the choice, as Wisconsin, Cleveland, and other jurisdictions have done for poor children in inner-city neighborhoods, and it explodes. Litigation is inevitable.

Debates over educational choice can be confusing. Arguments pro and con have a tendency to leave the discerning reader or listener with the impression that there is as much "choice" in selecting the appropriate meaning of the term "choice" as there is promise in the concept itself. It is only when an appropriate descriptive adjective defines the nature of the "choice" to be permitted that the contours of the debate—and its critical importance—become clear.

Viewed in historical, political, and sociological context, the debate over school choice is not really about "choice" at all. It is about *control*: of money, of curriculum content and viewpoint, and of teachers and how they teach.

The Function of Education

No one questions the assertion that education is, by its very nature, a value-laden process. Neither is there any argument with the proposition that education policy always raises questions important to both law and religion. When education is publicly-funded, it is only natural that disagreements over the place of religion in education tend to focus on questions of control. *Whose* values, *whose* perspectives concerning religion and its place in education, and *whose* religious practices shall be accommodated or preferred?

Controversies over whose religion should be accommodated in publicly-funded education have been with us since Colonial days. The earliest debates over parental choice in education date back to the period between 1810 and 1820. School choice issues are an archetypal illustration of the truth of the classic observation "*Plus ça change, plus c'ést la même chose.*"

For both the Jewish and Catholic communities, the generic Protestantism of the public schools was troubling. Both communities sought to be supportive of the goals of the common schools. Both desired a safe space where their children could grow and learn without fear of imposition, ridicule, or proselytization by adherents of other faiths. The common schools were not receptive to these concerns. They were hostile

Frustrated by the discrimination and animosity toward Catholics, the Church started its own school system in the mid-nineteenth century, and fought back attempts by Nativists and the Ku Klux Klan to shut it down in the 1920s. The Amish and other religious minorities responded in much the same manner, often (but not always) with much the same results.

Similar concerns have animated the educational strategies adopted by other minority communities. Wisconsin school choice pioneer Annette "Polly" Williams has argued for years that the Milwaukee public schools, its teacher unions, and other institutions of the state and local economic and political establishment ignore the interests of minority children as they pursue their self-interest.

The ongoing struggle of the Black community to achieve equality in education is, at bottom, a "school choice" problem. The issue in *Brown v. Board of Education* (1954) was segregation on the basis of race, a policy that limited equality and fostered racial animus by controlling the racial characteristics of the educational environment. Black students had no choice. Today there is a choice for students from upper and middle-class Black families, but poor children of all races are often trapped in public schools that do not meet their needs. And so the debate continues within the Black community concerning the wisdom and utility of "school choice" strategies as a means of furthering the economic and social welfare of children trapped in substandard inner-city and rural schools.

How will the law respond? There are three possible solutions. The first is to forbid any kind of voucher program, and to permit school choice only within the public school system. The second is to permit state aid to follow the child, and to impose no limit on the choice of an alternative school that otherwise meets the requirements of the compulsory education laws. The third option, viewed as a middle-ground by some, is to limit the choices of parents and children.

Each of these options is problematic.

Much has been said and written about the "public school only" option. It is the *status quo*. It is problematic for several reasons, not least of which is that it leaves the fate of children in the hands of school administrators, rather than parents. The ability of a poor child to choose a private school depends on private charity. To the extent that they exist at all, options among public schools are limited. In rural areas, there are often no alternative public schools to attend.

The "universal choice" option is criticized for leaving too much power in the hands of the parents, and for practical reasons. Not only are there not enough affordable private schools in operation, but the supply of currently available seats favors religiously-affiliated schools. Although Milwaukee's experimental program has been approved by the Wisconsin courts, it remains controversial. Children living outside of Milwaukee cannot participate, and only a limited number of children in the city are currently eligible. The inclusion of religious schools in the program also makes it inevitable that the judgement of the Wisconsin Supreme Court will be appealed to the United States Supreme Court.

The third option, viewed as a more "moderate" approach by some, would permit state funds to follow children to schools that do not teach from a religious perspective or include religion in their curriculum or activities. This option is discriminatory on its face. Exclusion of religious schools will inevitably result in litigation over the definition of "religion" and the degree to which it permeates a school's specific programs and activities.

In the end, however, these issues will not be resolved in the rough and tumble of the political process alone. Litigation is an inevitable part of the strategic equation, and the outcome will depend on how the United States Supreme Court reads the Religion Clause of the First Amendment.

The State of the Federal Case Law, Circa 1997
The First Amendment provides:

> Congress shall make no law respecting an establishment of religion, or prohibiting the free exercise thereof; or abridging the freedom of speech, or of the press; or the right of the people peaceably to assemble, and to petition the Government for a redress of grievances.

It is a truism among scholars of the First Amendment that the jurisprudence of the Religion Clause is a conceptual disaster area. Professors Mary Ann Glendon and Raul Yanes, among others, have urged both courts and scholars to undertake "a long overdue reconsideration of Religion Clause jurisprudence from the foundations." ("Structural Free Exercise," 90 Mich. L. Rev. 477, 547 (1991)). Recent case law indicates that the Court may be willing to reconsider its approach to questions arising under the Religion Clause. Should the Court be willing to undertake the task, school choice issues will provide the vehicle for that reconsideration.

Families and communities use both formal and informal education methods to transmit knowledge, culture, tradition, philosophy, and religion to their children. Education is accomplished by example, by use of the written and spoken word, and through socialization. It contains a variety of messages. Content and viewpoint are critical. Education cases thus stand at the intersection of all of the First Amendment's guarantees of non-establishment, free exercise, freedom of speech and of the press, peaceable assembly, and petition for redress of grievances.

Proverbs 22:6 admonishes us to "train up a child in the way he should go, and when he is old he will not depart from it." Education has been a key battleground of religious and academic freedom because every religious community in the United States takes those words to heart. All agree that protection of religious and academic freedom is (or should be) a key component of publicly-funded education programs. The disagreements center on matters of design and control.

Education cases having religious elements are usually described as "church-state cases." For analytical purposes, however, such cases can, and often do, raise a variety of related, but legally distinct, issues. Table One is a summary of the many ways that education cases having religious elements can be classified ("characterized") for purposes of legal analysis.

Table 1. Characterizing and Education Case Having Religious Elements

First Amendment Issues	Family Law Issues	Liberty or Equality Issues
non-establishment	custody	parental rights
free exercise	control	children's rights
speech and press	neglect	de jure and de facto discriminiation
assembly, association and non-association		academic freedom
petition for redress of grievances		

Each of these possible characterizations raises a distinct set of questions and constitutional issues. Family law, for example, requires that parents see to the education of their children. Parents who want significant control over the education of their children learn quickly, however, that professional educators control curriculum, environment, and child placement. A parent who objects, on grounds of religious liberty, to any aspect of the public education program thus faces a dilemma. Keeping the child from school until remedial action is taken can result in neglect charges, criminal prosecution under the compulsory education law, or loss of custody. Placing a child in private school requires a significant expenditure of money. Litigation designed to force recognition of parental concerns, including those centered on religious freedom, is often the only alternative.

A large body of state case law on what historians call the "School Question" has developed since the mid-nineteenth century. Federal case law concerning religion in education is of more recent vintage. Much of the public's understanding of the law of church-state relations is based on the holdings of the United States Supreme Court since 1947.

Table Two is a summary of the federal case law on support for students at religiously-affiliated school since 1947. This table should be viewed in light of several caveats. All but one are summarized below the table.

The first caveat relates to its content. Table Two contains only federal cases involving public support of religiously affiliated schools and their students decided since 1947. Federal cases dealing with religion in the public schools raise exactly the same issues, but are not included. State cases are excluded as well.

Everson v. Board of Education is the first case on the list. It marks the first time the United States Supreme Court applied the Establishment Clause to the States. It is also the first of its many subsequent attempts to convert Thomas Jefferson's metaphorical "Wall of Separation of Church and State" (derived from his famous Letter to the Danbury Baptists) into a rule of law.

However, as Jonathan Sarna points out elsewhere in this volume, the history of church-state disputes over education does not begin in 1947. It dates to the early nineteenth century. *Everson v. Board of Education* was not the first case on the subject of religion and education at the federal level, but it does lay down a basic federal "rule." State cases involving religious freedom in schools were in litigation nearly a century prior to Everson.

As the years have passed, the Court's attempts to construct a "wall of separation" between religion and publicly funded education have failed. What stands in its place is, by the Court's own admission, a "blurred, indistinct and variable barrier depending on all the circumstances of a particular relationship." (*Lynch v. Donnelly* (1984), quoting *Lemon v. Kurtzman* (1971)). The reason is straightforward: cases involving religion and education involve a wide range of constitutional issues and interests that cannot easily be reconciled.

Table Three is designed to illustrate kinds of federal constitutional questions that arise when taxpayers are asked to fund or support any type of educational program, public or private. The first column contains the constitutional provisions or doctrines most commonly raised in education cases. The second contains some of the questions a court considering a constitutional case arising under that particular clause will have to answer.

The questions presented in Table Three demonstrate why the Court is thus caught on the horns of a dilemma of its own making. A "no aid" rule is easy to administer, and would be consistent with the "strict separation" view of the Establishment Clause. The values protected by the Free Exercise, Speech and Press, Petition, and Equal Protection Clauses would simply be subordinated to the "no-aid" principle. A set of rulings that accommodates religious belief, speech, and practice in the context of publicly funded education, would necessarily result in a scaling back of the Court's commitment to a regime of "strict separation."

Table 2. The Supreme Court on support for Students Enrolled at Religiously Affiliated Schools (1947–1997)

Case	Permits	Forbids	Reason
Everson v. Bd. of Ed. 330 U.S. 1 (1947)	Reimbursement to parents of transportation costs		Generally available, neutral public welfare program for children
Bd. of Ed. v. Allen 392 U.S. 236 (1968)	Loan of Secular Textbooks		Aid to children
Walz v. Tax Comm'n 397 U.S. 664 (1970)	Tax Exemptions		No First Amendment violation
Lemon v. Kurtzman 403 U.S. 602 (1971)	Loan of Secular Textbooks	Teacher Salary Supplements	Excessive administrative entanglement
Tilton v. Richardson 403 U.S. 672 (1971)	Grants to religiously-affiliated college under federal program supporting construction of college facilities used for secular purposes		Schools were not "pervasively sectarian," college students are less susceptible to religious indoctrination than younger children, and nature of aid did not lead to excessive entanglement
Hunt v. McNair	use of state bonding authority to finance secular program facilities at religiously affiliated colleges		School was not so sectarian as to make it impossible to separate religious and secular components of its program
Comm. for Public Ed. v. Nyquist		Tuition tax credit to parents	Aids religion, Catholic schools primary beneficiary
Sloan v. Lemon 413 U.S. 756 (9173)		Tuition reimbursement to parents	Aids religion, Catholic schools primary beneficiary

Table 2. The Supreme Court on support for Students Enrolled at Religiously Affiliated Schools (1947–1997) cont.

Case	Permits	Forbids	Reason
Levitt v. Comm. for Pub. Ed. 413 U.S. 472 (1973)		Per capita reimbursement to school of state-mandated service costs	Aids religion, no guarantee that aid would be used to defray only secular costs
Meek v. Pittenger 421 U.S. 349 (1975)	Loan of Secular Textbooks		Approved in *Allen*
		On-premises educational services by public school personnel	Possibility that public school teachers might advance religious mission
		Loan of instructional materials, such as maps, globes, A.V. equipment	Aids religious mission by making schools more viable
Roemer v. Bd of Public Works 426 U.S. 736 (1976)	Annual per-student subsidy to private universities amounting to 15% of the aid given to students in state institutions		Institutions were not so "evasively sectarian" as to make it impossible to separate religious and secular components of the education program
Wolman v. Walter 433 U.S. 229 (1977)		Cost of bus transportation to field trips	Might advance religious mission
	Off premises diagnostic/remedial services		No possible religious effect
	Loan of secular textbooks		Approved in *Allen*
	Funds to distribute and score standardized tests used in public schools		Important secular purpose, no religious involvement in preparation of tests
		Loan of instruction materials	Might advance religious mission
New York v. Cathedral Academy 434 U.S. 125 (1977)		Reimbursement to schools under program held invalid in Levitt	Advances religion, fostered excessive entanglement. Reliance on program by schools prior to challenge irrelevant.

Table 2. The Supreme Court on support for Students Enrolled at Religiously Affiliated Schools (1947–1997) cont.

Case	Permits	Forbids	Reason
Comm. for Public Ed v. Regan 444 U.S. 646 (1980)	Reimbursement to school for standardized testing and reporting services		No religious effect. Repaid only administrative costs
Mueller v. Allen 421 U.S. 349 (1983)	Tax deduction for parents educational expenses at any school		
Witters v. Wash. Dept. Serv. for the Blind 474 U.S. 481 (1986)	Tuition at school of handicapped college student's choice		College student had right to choose and program was neutral.
Aguilar v. Felton 473 U.S. 402 (1985)		On-premises remedial education for poor children	No guarantee that public officials would not advance religious mission of the school. *Aguilar* was overruled in 1997 in *Agostini v. Felton*.
Ball v. School. Dist. of Grand Rapids 473 U.S. 373 (1985)		"Shared time" public school teachers teaching secular subjects on private school premises	Frees up resources for religious function; creates "symbolic" link between church and state.
Bowen v. Kendrick 484 U.S. 942 (1987)	Grants to churches and religious institutions to develop secular sex education programs approved by federal government		Religious institutions may participate in general social welfare programs, but may not utilize funds to advance religion.
Zobrest v. Catalina School District 509 U.S. 1 (1993)	On-premises sign-language interpreter for deaf child in religious secondary school		Benefits available in otherwise neutral program
Agostini v. Felton 117 S.Ct. 1997 (1997)	On-premises remedial education for poor children		Benefits available in otherwise neutral program

Table 3: A Typology of School Choice Cases and Constitutional Questions Presented

Case Type, by Clause	Questions Raised
Establishment Clause	Does the Establishment Clause permit, or require, federal control of the religious content or viewpoint of education purchased with public funds?
Free Exercise Clause	To what extent will religion, religious exercise, and religious speech (including proselytization) be accommodated in public settings, including the public schools?
Speech and Press Clause	To what extent do the guarantees of freedom of speech and of the press limit the government's ability to control the content or perspective of the speech, or of the written work of teachers and students, in publicly funded educational programs?
Peaceable Assembly	To what extent may the government limit the ability of groups to assemble peaceably on public property, including public school buildings?
Petition for Redress of Grievances	To what extent does the First Amendment limit the range of possible legislative outcomes available to political factions aggrieved by the government's claim that it may control the content, viewpoint, and environment of educational programs purchased with public funds?
Parental Control	To what extent does the Constitution protect and preserve the primary right of parents to control over the education and socialization of their children?
Liberty (Substantive Due Process)	To what extent does the Constitution's guarantee that "liberty" will not be taken without "due process of law" limit the government's ability to restrict individual and parental choices among educational alternatives?
Equality	Do the Constitution's guarantees of equal protection of the law, including the No Religious Test Clause of Article VI, permit public funding of "common schools" only, or can they also be construed to permit the funding of private and religious schools as well?

A good example of the inverse relationship between "strict separation" and other constitutional values is illustrated by the Court's decision in *Aguilar v. Felton*. In *Aguilar*, the purpose of the litigation was to eliminate on-site remedial education services for poor children who attend religious schools. Although no public assistance actually flowed to the religious schools, a majority of the Court thought that the program itself created a "symbolic link" between church and state that should be eliminated. The intended effect of the decision was to compel poor children entitled to services to go to the public schools in order to get them.

Agostini v. Felton, which reverses *Aguilar,* adopts an approach described by Dr. Sarna as "equal footing." After *Agostini,* children are entitled to on-site remedial education services provided by public school teachers, regardless of the religious or non-religious character of the school they attend. The dissenting Justices in Agostini objected. In their view, the Court's approach is a breach in the "wall of separation."

The final caveat concerning Table Two is contextual. The table is a summary of the holdings of a shifting majority of the United States Supreme Court concerning the types of aid permitted or forbidden at any point in time. It cannot possibly capure the political dynamics that led to litigation over the specific types of aid in issue, and is affected by changes in the membership of the United States Supreme Court.

Taken as a whole, Table Two is a reflection of the political battles that led to the adoption of the challenged aid programs. The case law addressing the "School Question" is not a set of rules derived from a dispassionate reading of the constitutional text. The United States Constitution says nothing about education, either public or private. The outcomes are compromises, and the rules are designed to permit the Court to strike what Justice Sandra Day O'Connor has called "sensible balances" between and among the interests of the competing political factions. (See *Employment Div. v. Smith* (1990), O'Connor concurring.) These "balances" shape our understanding of the meaning of the First Amendment, but they are incomprehensible unless there is some understanding of the political, religious, and philosophical differences among the contending factions.

Controversies over aid to private schools and battles over the content or perspective of public school programs revolve around a set of common questions: "How, and in what setting, shall the community's children be educated?" Political disagreements over immigration policy, cultural and linguistic assimilation, the role of religion in education, the rights and obligations of religious and political minorities, and political control of culture-forming institutions are as important today as they were in the period before the Civil War.

In Table Four (p. 77) the focus is the factional interests that complicate controversies over taxpayer-funded school choice programs. It builds on the questions raised in Table Three by contrasting the factional interests involved when the federal courts consider school finance questions.

The first column heading is *Parent & Student "First Amendment" Interests.* Each of these interests described under that heading is recognized as a "first amendment interest" by the United States Supreme Court, and would merit significant protection were the funds supporting an educational program to be derived purely from private sources. Parents and students who want an equal share of public assistance devoted to education of the community's children assert these interests. So do their opponents.

The second column heading is *Taxpayer "First Amendment" Interests.* In that column are summarized the interests of two distinct sets of taxpayers. The first group includes those who object to the use of their tax money to support educational programs that offer educational content with which they disagree. For purposes of this discussion, it also includes taxpayers that support the ideal of a common school system, and who believe that private schooling fosters the social, religious, and economic fragmentation of the community. The case law often refers to these individuals as "*dissenting* taxpayers." So too does Table Four.

Table Four uses the term "*supportive* taxpayers" to describe taxpayers who agree with the use of their tax dollars to support a wide range of religious, philosophical and political perspectives in educational programs. Taxpayers that do not object to the use of public funds to pay for education in private schools are included in this category by default.

The political debate over public financing of education at private schools pits at least these three—and usually many more—political factions against each other. If a legislature decides to provide funds to defray all or part of the cost of private education, it can safely be assumed that the supportive taxpayer faction prevailed in the legislature. When a "supportive" bill reaches the executive (Governor or President) for signature or veto, the lobbying for a result deemed favorable inevitably involves the same political factions.

Factional involvement does not change after a case goes to court, but the dynamics change considerably. The legislative process is a "give-and-take," where compromise is the essence of good policy-making. In litigation over the "School Question," however, the allegation is that taxpayer support of education having religious elements is not simply unwise; it is *unconstitutional*. The goal is "winner-take-all," and the rhetoric is phrased in the language of high constitutional principle.

The United States Supreme Court has built much of its jurisprudence of the Religion Clause on the premise that it is the job of the federal courts to strike "sensible balances" between and among competing factional interests in education cases. In order to facilitate that role and encourage litigation, the Court has made it easy for dissenting taxpayers to challenge payments to, or on behalf of, children enrolled in religious schools.

And what makes a balance "sensible"? In the view of the Court and most legal and political commentators, a major concern is the way in which the outcome affects the interests of "minorities." Where the issue is school finance policy, the Court will seek to determine "who benefits?", and will scrutinize closely any program that seems discriminatory in either design or operation.

Table Five looks at the same factional interests summarized in Table Four, column one, but compares them with the interests of factions that are concerned that funding programs will either discriminate against their children, or leave them at a disadvantage.

The questions raised in Table Five (p. 78) are central to the resolution of many of the cases mentioned in Table One. They are also important variables in the cases omitted from that table: *i.e.* those involving religion in the public schools.

Concluding Observations

Writing in another context, Justice Sandra Day O'Connor has observed that the Supreme Court's case law was "on a collision course with itself." The Court's jurisprudence of the First Amendment suffers from the same problem.

It is possible—perhaps likely—that the current political debate over "school choice" will culminate in a series of cases that will give the Court the opportunity to clarify just how much parental and student choice in elementary and secondary education the First Amendment permits. Until those cases go to final judgment in the United States Supreme Court, however, advocates for and against school vouchers will be able to read the case law both ways.

A well-constructed school choice program that permits funded choice of a religious school might survive a constitutional challenge. It might not. The best that can be said at present is that the issue is a political one: in the states, in the Congress, and, unfortunately, in the courts. In the end, the issue will ultimately be decided the old-fashioned way: by counting the votes.

In closing, let me urge that all who reflect on this issue consider the admonition of Judge John T. Noonan, Jr. of the United States Court of Appeals for the Ninth Circuit. Only when we "immerse ourselves in history" will we be able to "appropriat[e] the experience that undergirds the constitutional principles of free exercise and no establishment."[1] In order to understand why school choice is such an important issue today, we need to understand the historical factors that prompted religious minorities to fight so hard to preserve educational choices for themselves and their children.

Endnotes

1. John T. Noonan, Jr. *The Beliver and the Powers That Are*, (Macmillan 1987), p. xiii.

Table 4. Interests Affected by Public Funding of Education Having Religious Elements

(Limited to consideration of Parent/Student and Taxpayer "First Amendment" interests)

Parent & Student "First Amendment" Interests	Taxpayer "First Amendment" Interests	
Free exercise of religion: Freedom to choose an educational program consistent with religious and moral beliefs, needs, and practices	Dissenting taxpayers	Non-association with ideas or beliefs
	Supportive taxpayers	Civic recognition of the value of different perspectives on educational matters
Free speech and press. Freedom to choose teachers, teaching materials, and textbooks that are consistent with religious, moral, and philosophical beliefs.	Dissenting taxpayers	Non-association with ideas or beliefs contrary to taxpayer's own. Lack of community control of the content or perspective of the prescribed curriculum.
	Supportive taxpayers	Civic recognition that eduction is not value-neutral, and that all teaching proceeds from a moral and political "perspective" on "the good."
Freedom to assemble peaceably, to associate freely, and to determine the terms of that association in a manner consistent with the law.	Dissenting taxpayers	Avoidance of religious factionalism, or political division along religious and other ideological lines concerning the content of education.
	Supportive taxpayers	Encouragement of diverse cultural, religious and intellectual educational resources.
The right to petition for redress of financial grievances caused by funding schemes that prefer one viewpoint on learning over others.	Dissenting taxpayers	Fear that political majorities will impose their religiously-motivated views of the common good on dissenters, including the possibility that there will be no secular alternative to religious education.
	Supportive taxpayers	Vindication of majoritarian democracy and representative government fostering parental choice.

Table 5. Interests Affected by Public funding of Education Having Religious Elements

(Limited to consideration of Parent/Student interests from a Minority/Majority religious perspective)

Parent/Student Interests	"Practical" Concerns of Majority/Minority Faith Groups	
Free exercise of religion: Freedom to choose an educational program consistent with religious and moral beliefs, needs, and practices	Minority faiths	How will minority faiths, especially small ones, find adequate educational program alternatives? Will the alternative education programs available be equal in quality or diversity to meet their needs? Will funding, facilities, or other resources be allocated on an equal basis?
	Majority faiths	How will disputes be resolved concerning the allocation of resources between and among the education programs competing for public funds?
Free speech and press. Freedom to choose teachers, teaching materials, and textbooks that are consistent with religious, moral, and philosophical beliefs.	Minority faiths	Will competing programs be available? Can proselytism be avoided in programs controlled by others? How can adherents of minority faiths control the content or perspective of the curriculum to which their children are exposed?
	Majority faiths	Is it possible to avoid disputes among religious factions concerning the choice of materials, the tone and content of curricula, and the selection of teachers?
Freedom to assemble peaceably, to associate freely, and to determine the terms of that association in a manner consistent with the law.	Minority faiths	How can adherents of minority faiths avoid discrimination in, or exclusion from, educational programs funded by community resources. Is it possible, or wise, to resist public pressure to de-emphasize the unique religious identities of religious schools that accept public funds?
	Majority faiths	Why should the public fund educational programs that will not appeal to the general public, and that may discriminate on the basis of religion?
The right to petition for redress of financial grievances caused by funding schemes that prefer one viewpoint on learning over others.	Minority faiths	How can adherents of minority religions recapture their state-law entitlements to funding of educational programs for children? How can schools adhering to a minority religious viewpoint avoid public pressure to de-emphasize their religious identity after having accepted public funds?
	Majority faiths	Why should the public fund educational programs that will not appeal to the general public, and that may discriminate on the basis of religion? Is it possible to maintain the funding advantages built into the current system of school finance?

Remarks From a Roundtable

Marc Stern
There are a number of ways we could discuss the issue of vouchers here. The primary focus of this panel is going to be on church-state separation, which I frankly regard as something of a "red herring" in regard to the current debates. I do not believe that the contemporary political impetus for vouchers has very much to do with debates over the exact boundary between church and state.

In part the impetus is impatience in inner-city communities with public schools that have failed. As far as I know, there is no data indicating that choice is preferred in those communities over institutions that work, but until they do work, vouchers will be attractive. Nevertheless, I think that the bulk of the current political impetus for vouchers around the country is an effort to deconstruct (not in the academic sense of the word, but in the sense to "tear down") the role of government as a provider of social services, and particularly, educational services. The movement for vouchers stems from a libertarian economic and political outlook that has very little in common with the debate over church-state separation. So, while I would rather discuss policy, I'll stick to the assigned topic of Constitutional Law.

The strongest arguments against voucher proposals lie in state constitutional provisions which require states to operate public schools and to ensure that tax funds go only to public schools. Those are not exclusively motivated by church-state concerns, but also by a democratic commitment to schools operated by the government, subject to democratic control, with the purpose of serving as common schools. Common schools serve two functions. First, they provide a common curriculum across the state to everybody who wants it—and the framers of these provisions *thought* that most children would attend them. And along with useful knowledge and useful skills, common schools teach adherence to an agreed upon set of civic values.

Second, (and this is little noticed, although I notice it as a parent who sends his kids to yeshiva) these schools serve as a sort of mark against which every school must measure the education it provides. With the exception of schools operated by fairly small separatist groups, private and public schools compete for students. If the public schools set a particular agenda and offer particular skills, particular bodies of knowledge, and particular values, then every other school in the society, as a practical matter, has to hold in large measure to those common values. That would not be the case if a voucher plan destroys, as it would, the special role of the public schools. So under the state constitutions there is, in addition to the church-state issue, a question of the role of the public school.

So I think that the key issue that we discuss in vouchers is whether there is a role for government here—whether government ought to be the primary setter of values, and whether it ought to have a role in holding everybody else toward some sort of center. In a free country the government should not be the educator, though you do want some system to set the norm.

In church-state separation terms, the division is between four Justices who would probably uphold vouchers, and four Justices who would not, with the decision in the hands of Justice O'Connor. (Eugene Gressman told me last week that somebody was once faced with a similar problem in another case. Four Justices thought one thing, four Justices thought the opposite, and Justice Stewart was on the fence. A lawyer got up to argue and he said, "Well, Justice Stewart, I might as well just direct this to you and see if I can persuade you." Justice Stewart's response was, "In that case, you'll lose eight to one.") There are two theories now on the Court about the Establishment Clause. We do not need to bother with details beyond knowing that these are the broad visions that exist. The first vision, which has been the view that has animated the Court since 1947 (and some state courts even before that) is that the Establishment Clause is a form of legalized discrimination against religion. That is, the Constitution imposes special restrictions on what government may do for religion—particularly, in regard to finance and, more particularly, with regard to educational finance. There was a good deal of public discussion in the nineteenth century about the Establishment Clause which lends credence to that view—for instance, Judge Cooley's *Constitutional Treatise* in the late nineteenth century. Similarly, the Judge Black who wrote the dictionary that all of us lugged around in our first year of law school, also wrote a book in the 1890s (one which is, thankfully for Professor Rotunda, now forgotten) in which he managed to get all of constitutional law into one volume. He states as a principle that, "the government may not fund any religious enterprise." So that is one vision of church-state separation of the Establishment Clause.

The second view, which has become prominent among the conservatives on the court in recent years, is that the Establishment Clause is a sort of a nondiscrimination clause. You can't favor religion, but neither are you permitted to discriminate against it. If government treats religion equally with comparable secular ideological views and institutions, it can fund religious institutions—even explicitly religious undertakings. That is the great debate that I see in the Court. Even as it has edged on occasion—in cases like *Rosenberg, Witters* and *Bowen*—towards the equal treatment analysis, the Court has always stopped short. There has always been something out there that has held it back. In *Bowen*, for example, the Court said, "Yes, you can fund religious institutions equally with secular institutions, provided they don't actually teach religion." But if one accepts an equal treatment theory, there's no reason for that caveat.

In the speech context, where the Court has bought the equal treatment argument entirely, there can be no restrictions at all on the religious content of privately sponsored speech. In funding, there has been this reluctance to adopt the argument. If you look at all the cases, that has been precisely the point on which the Court has divided. It is most clearly marked in the case of *Mueller v. Allen*, where equal treatment for the first time gets adopted by a majority of the Court. That was followed a year or two later by a case called *Witters v. Washington Department of Services for the Blind*. Witters was a blind fellow who wanted to take advantage of rehabilitation funds to go to a theological school. The Washington state courts had invalidated the program on Establishment Clause grounds. When the case came to the Supreme Court, it was reversed. The majority pointedly ignored Mueller and its equal treatment theory. Justice Powell, even though concurring, said, "I don't know why you'd write this long opinion. *Mueller v. Allen* and its equality theory is a total answer." That's the break that you've got in the Court. When and if that battle gets resolved in the Supreme Court (and they have been battling it for over a decade now), we will know where we stand with vouchers.

The Free Exercise Clause does not really change this analysis very much. If you listen to the arguments for vouchers, they essentially boil down to the claim, first of all, that the current system is not fair in taxing parents to pay for public education and not helping with tuition. That's the fundamental public choice you have to make about whether religion ought to be subject to special restraints or not. The second argument—the one that I have the hardest time with—is that there are some public schools in this country that simply don't work and don't educate. That's Polly Williams' argument for vouchers. It's very different, for example, than Milton Friedman's argument. That's the hardest argument to deal with. We ought to be able to address the question—no, we have to address the question—of non-functioning public schools in the inner city. But I don't know why that should require a revolution in the Establishment Clause jurisprudence.

Ronald Rotunda

I think there are two important cases in this whole debate. The first is *Committee on Public Education v. Nyquist*. In 1973 the Supreme Court said it was unconstitutional to give tax credits to people going to private schools, which were primarily Catholic. We have to realize, however, that if tax credits were allowed, we would find more schools, with more diversity, opening up all the time. There would be other religious schools, there would be military schools, there would be schools emphasizing the dance or a foreign language. Then in 1983, in a second case, *Mueller v. Allen*, the Supreme Court said it was alright to give tax deductions. So when we put these two cases together, it turns out that we can give tax *deductions* to people who choose to send their children to private schools (whether religiously affiliated or not), but we can't give them tax *credits*. So what the Supreme Court is telling us is that it's alright for the state or the federal government to subsidize private K–12 as long as they do it in a way that helps rich people more than poor people. If you wind up doing it in a way that helps all people the same, God forbid, that's unconstitutional. I find that bizarre.

Both cases—one from New York, the other from Minnesota—were based on the Fourteenth Amendment Due Process Clause. When our soldiers fought in the Civil War, the big legacy of that was the Fourteenth Amendment. If we count the dead of all the American wars up to, but not including, the Vietnam War, we find that we lost more soldiers in the Civil War than all the other American wars combined. And what were they fighting for? To make sure that if we aid private education, we do it in a way that it helps rich people more than poor people? I don't understand that.

As Marc Stern pointed out, we can give public money to religiously affiliated universities like this one (Catholic University) or Notre Dame or to a Baptist college (in *Hunt v. McNair*, the Supreme Court permitted financing bonds for a Baptist college). We can give it to a higher education that does nothing but produce missionaries (*Witters v. Washington Dept. of Services for the Blind*) But we can't give it to K–12.

We ought to be able to have, as a constitutional matter, tax credits or vouchers—and a voucher system is even more fair, because it would also help the poorest of our people, those who pay no taxes. We can do it now as long as we give it to any private school *except* a religious school. So it seems we can do it only in a way that hurts religious education. Now, if it takes the public school, say $6,000 to educate a child (taking state and local aid together), you would think that if you gave a private school a voucher for less than $6,000 ($5,000, say, or $2,000, or 95 percent of that $6,000), then not one penny of it would be going to religious education because the state has already told us it takes at least $6,000 just to give them their secular education!

We talk about experiments. We already have an experiment. It's called college. We have both public and private colleges. The private colleges are both religiously affiliated and not religiously affiliated. Harvard gets a huge chunk of its money from the federal government. The University of Illinois gets less than half of its budget from the state. In many ways, the University of Illinois is as private as Harvard. Higher education can get all kinds of money from the federal government, and a private school can as well—even if it's Notre Dame.

There is no doubt that if there were no state aid to private colleges, the public universities would not be as good as they are today, and professors who teach there would be paid less. The advantage of private competition is that if one school isn't doing a good job educating its students, parents will pull their children out and put them in another school that does it better. Obviously any state which had vouchers would forbid racial segregation in the public schools—that would be constitutionally required.

If we had such a voucher system, we would have much more intellectual diversity than we have now. And we would give all parents, including poor parents, the same right that Chelsea Clinton's parents had—the right to choose a private school education.

Professor Lester Thurow of MIT was recently talking on PBS on why we shouldn't worry about our education. What he said was interesting. He claimed that on the international level we have the best higher education in the world. People come here from all over the globe to attend our universities. He admitted that our K–12 is not nearly as good, but said that they "catch up by the time they go to college." I like to call him "Less Thorough." If we could make K–12 much better, why do we say we shouldn't bother because those who can afford to go to universities can catch up, and those who can't afford to go to universities never catch up? What we ought to do, I think, is give all people the same economic opportunity that only rich people have now.

Sanford Levinson

I agree with Marc Stern than any reasonably competent lawyer can design an argument on either side of this, or for that matter, almost any, issue involving the interplay of church and state. This is especially the case where, as with the voucher issue, the argument can plausibly be made that any Establishment Clause concern is more than counterbalanced by the legitimate interest of the state in making possible the effective free exercise of one's religious commitments to educate one's children and thus attempt to maintain the religious community across time. Moreover, as a practical matter, the success or failure of these arguments, especially at the level of the United States Supreme Court, may well depend on future appointments to be made by President Clinton and his successor. No Justice, for example, is more likely to be hostile to voucher plans than Justice Stevens, but he is also getting up in years and likely to retire before the issue is "definitively" resolved (assuming the Court ever does such a thing). His replacement will be, almost by definition, more open-minded on the issue and could turn out to provide a fifth vote, assuming there aren't already five votes to allow wide-scale latitude on the issue. In any event, I doubt that it's particularly useful to spend our time guessing what the Supreme Court will do.

What I would like to do, far too briefly, is to comment on something that I find much more interesting than the parsing of Supreme Court opinions. This is the fact that many of the arguments for vouchers, including the ones presented today by Ron Rotunda and Representative Williams, seem far closer to classic liberal Democratic arguments than to "conservative" ones, even though the voucher issue is often described as a conservative one. If I am right, this suggests two things: a) there is more room for classic coalition building than might otherwise have been suspected, and b) there may be some instability in the argument itself, in that some conservative supporters of vouchers might indeed turn out to be highly uncomfortable at certain of the reasons offered by their putative allies.

Both Ron Rotunda and Representative Williams presented what I think can fairly be termed a classic egalitarian argument that the less well-off should have (relatively speaking) the same options as the better-off in regard to school choice. If they (the less well-off) do not have the material resources (*i.e.*, money) to buy the kind of schools they prefer through the market system, then the state should act so as to provide the resources and, therefore, the effective opportunity to choose the schools they think best for their children. I have publicly indicated that my own views on the voucher issue were turned around several years ago by reading a brilliant article by Michael McConnell ("The Selective Funding Problem: Abortions and Religious Schools," 104 *Harvard Law Review* 989 [1991]), in which he said, in effect, that if one is a liberal Democrat, as I unrepentantly am, and support, for example, state-funded abortion, on the grounds that poor women should not be barred effectively from being able to purchase something of such fundamental importance to their lives, then it is anomalous, to say the least, that the same liberal Democrats so insistently oppose subsidies for the less well-off in regard to religious schools, especially given that the Constitution even more clearly protects the free exercise of religion than it does abortion. (Michael, of course, would not concede that it protects abortion at all, but, as I say, he was challenging liberals to live up to their own egalitarian doctrines.) I decided that he was right. But the important thing is that he was doing a kind of jujitsu insofar as he was using basically liberal egalitarian arguments against liberal Democrats themselves. There was, that is, nothing truly "conservative" in the argument. I would hope that my fellow liberal Democrats would be more open to the McConnell-Rotunda-Williams kind of argument, but the real question is ultimately whether the contemporary Republican party of Richard Armey and other radical anti-egalitarian freemarketers can possibly be comfortable with such arguments.

As I've already hinted, one can easily imagine other Democrats joining Representatives Williams and Flake in supporting school vouchers, even if they are less enthusiastic about vouchers than are these Representatives. Perhaps they should demand as a price that Republican adherents of vouchers live up to their new-found egalitarianism by revisiting some of the most egregiously laissez-faire, anti-egalitarian features of the so-called welfare "reforms" of 1996. I would make such a deal in a minute. Would Republican supporters of vouchers, such as J. C. Watt, agree to any such deals? If not, this suggests that the egalitarianism stated in behalf of vouchers is more opportunistic than principled.

A second argument in behalf of vouchers, made especially by Ron Rotunda, involves protecting diversity, or—dare one say it?—multiculturalism. Again, defenses of multiculturalism are more likely to be found on the left than on the right. Yet, as I've just suggested, many of the strongest arguments for school choice are precisely the same sorts of arguments one hears from self-described multiculturalists. That is, one can easily argue that there has been way too much emphasis on socializing the young into one common cook-cut melting-pot, etc. One ought, instead, to recognize that we are a great, vast land of very, very different peoples; and parents may legitimately wish to have their children maintain their specific culture across the generations, whether or not it's a culture that coexists very easily with other parts of our society.

Sometimes one hears school choice defended in terms of how this will help strengthen us as a republic, but in all candor, I don't think that protecting the rights of the Satmar Hasidim, to pick one group entirely non-randomly, has anything at all to do with strengthening us as a generally democratic society or preserving the United States as a "republican" political community. As Montesquieu argued several centuries ago, "the love of one's country...is not a moral, but a political virtue, and it is the spring which sets the republican government in motion." The Satmars, so far as I know, have no "love" for the United States, the very notion of which probably (and maybe even justifiably) sounds idolatrous; nor do I imagine them having even any interest in what the Constitution deems the "general," as opposed to partial, welfare of the

American polity. Their citizenship in the United States is formal only; their most basic loyalties are to their particular community. So be it. (I suspect the same is largely true of the Old Order Amish or the Jehovah's Witnesses, other frequent participants in church-state cases and favorite examples of academics on both sides of the argument.)

What justifies acquiescing to certain desires of the Satmars or the Amish is not the health of the United States as a polity, but, rather, the basic value of accommodating a highly deviant social group (and I use "deviant" in an entirely non-pejorative statistical sense) in its desire to maintain its very unusual way of life across time. Again, as I have said, these sorts of arguments (including the dismissal of standard "patriotic" considerations of molding national loyalties and the like) are more often found on the left than on the right, though, interestingly enough, several analysts identified with the left, including, for example, Todd Gitlin, have eloquently criticized the left's repudiation of "common dreams" and their too-easy endorsement of what has come to be called "identity politics." Still, if one is concerned about coalition-building, then many of the adherents of school vouchers, especially Evangelical Christians, should more openly admit to adopting multiculturalist arguments, however much that might embarrass them to admit it. Though, again, one wonders if such admissions would break some of the alliances with the right. Presumably this is something that the tacticians fighting in behalf of school vouchers must decide for themselves.

I also want to mention a third issue relating to vouchers, in which the proponents might find themselves in what they regard as unexpected company. It is no secret that the contemporary Republican Party has wrapped itself around the Tenth Amendment and a form of states-rights federalism that would have made John Calhoun and Jefferson Davis proud. Yet consider an argument made in a superb article, which Marshall Breger drew to my attention, by Professor Joseph P. Viteritti ("Choosing Equality: Religious Freedom and Educational Opportunity Under Constitutional Federalism," 15 *Yale Law and Policy Review* 113 [1996]). One of his main points is that the national Constitution might turn out, in many states, to be a relatively minor player in the overall game of school vouchers. Why is this the case? The answer is easy: many state constitutions have "Establishment Clause-like" provisions that have been interpreted even more strictly than has the Establishment Clause of the First Amendment. After all, consider the fact that the cases discussed today from Wisconsin and Ohio were decided not under the U.S. Constitution, but, rather, under their respective state constitutions. Wisconsin and Ohio are certainly not unique. Thus Professor Viteritti calls for a highly aggressive, nationalist reading of the Fourteenth Amendment that would basically invalidate all of the state constitutional limitations on the use of public funds for any sort of aid, including "indirect" aid, of religious schools. The Supreme Court should declare that such state constitutional provisions violate the Free Exercise Clause. There is nothing silly about such an argument; all of us on this panel could write a brief arguing this, whether or not, as a final matter, we were persuaded that it was in fact the "best" reading of the Constitution. My major point, though, is that this argument requires supporting a remarkable degree of judicial activism in striking down the ability of a "sovereign state" to make its own decision (whether wise or not is not the main point right now) as to how much intermingling of general public funds with religious institutions it wishes to allow. To put it mildly, I believe that Justice Scalia, usually counted a warm supporter of the constitutionality of state accommodation, would recoil from the kind of activism that some of his putative allies seem to be calling for.

In any event, I hope it is clear that it is very hard these days to tell the politics of the players arguing for school vouchers without a scorecard. If one has certain stereotypical notions of what it means these days to make a "right wing" or "left wing" argument, one may well be unprepared for the actual, and extremely interesting, debate that is swirling around the topic.

Agostini and the Politics of the Establishment Clause

Robert Destro

Background and Introduction

Agostini v. Felton (1997) is the most recent case in which the United States Supreme Court has considered how, and under what circumstances, it will permit state and federal financial aid for students attending schools which have a religious perspective. At issue were provisions of Title I of the Elementary and Secondary Education Act of 1965 that require local educational agencies (LEAs) to provide remedial education services to all eligible children. Under Title I, children who attend private schools are entitled to services that are "equitable in comparison to services and other benefits for public school children." It falls upon the LEAs to design and implement remedial education programs that comply with this mandate.

Agostini tells the story of how one LEA, the Board of Education of the City of New York, was trapped in an ongoing, high-stakes political and legal struggle over the distribution of federal education finance dollars. On one side of this struggle are children who attend schools that teach from a religious perspective, their taxpaying parents, non-public school administrators and teachers, and the religious organizations that sponsor schools. On the other side are organizations representing the interests of parents and children attending public schools, public school teachers and administrators, and individual taxpayers and organizations that object to any taxpayer financing of private education, especially if it has a discernable religious perspective.

The inclusion of funds for the support of children attending private and religiously affiliated schools in the provisions of the Elementary and Secondary School Act (ESEA) was a major political loss for the "no-aid" faction. They had only one avenue left: constitutional litigation designed to enshrine the "no-aid" position in the United States Constitution.

The premise that constitutional amendment was the only way to eliminate or avoid political gains by the factions supporting children in non-public schools was the basis of the political strategies of factions opposing religiously-affiliated schools during the period from 1865 to 1889. An attempt to amend the federal Constitution to prohibit any form of aid to nonpublic schools, dubbed the "Blaine Amendment" after its chief sponsor James G. Blaine, was attempted, but failed in 1875. If the "no-aid" position of the failed Blaine Amendment was to be enshrined in the Constitution, the Court would have to accomplish that goal by holding that the "no-aid" position was required by the First Amendment. Therefore litigation challenging the constitutionality of ESEA began almost immediately after its passage, with the goal of "constitutionalizing" the "no-aid" position, and thereby eliminating any possibility of either federal or state aid to nonpublic schools.

The litigation specific to the dispute in *Agostini* began in 1978 when a group of taxpayers sought and obtained an injunction that prohibited the Board of Education

> "from using public funds for any plan or program under (Title 1) to the extent that it requires, authorizes or permits public school teachers and guidance counselors to provide teaching and counseling services on the premises of sectarian schools within New York City."

The United States Supreme Court affirmed this injunction in *Aguilar v. Felton* (1985). In the view of the five-Justice *Aguilar* majority, it is unconstitutional for Congress to allocate remedial education assistance funds for children enrolled in schools that have discernable religious perspectives in their curricula. The majority gave three reasons:

1. "(F)irst, state-paid teachers conducting classes in the sectarian environment might inadvertently (or intentionally) manifest sympathy with the sectarian aims (of the school) to the point of using public funds for religious educational purposes,"
2. "Second, the government's provision of secular instruction in religious schools produced a symbolic union of church and state that tended to convey a message to students and to the public that the State supported religion," and
3. "(F)inally, the . . . program subsidized the religious functions of the religious schools by assuming responsibility for teaching secular subjects the schools would otherwise be required to provide."

The Legal and Political Importance of *Agostini*

The importance of *Agostini* is both legal and political. After *Agostini*, plaintiffs who want to challenge programs providing educational assistance to children attending religious schools must find and produce evidence that the programs they oppose are operated in a manner that violates the First Amendment. It thus strikes a balance between the First Amendment and substantive due process rights of plaintiffs and the statutory and procedural due process rights of the beneficiaries of these programs.

The Court's determination to rely on adjudicative facts is politically significant as well. The thorny political nature of the "School Question" was apparent as early as the early 1800s, and it can only be resolved on a level political playing field. Until *Agostini*, the Court's "School aid" jurisprudence rested on sociological, political and demographic data—"social facts." Wittingly or unwittingly, the Court has created the impression that Establishment Clause litigation is "a continuation of cultural politics by other means."[1] Worse, it often appears implacably hostile to elementary and secondary educational programs having a religious perspective—especially when their sponsors are Catholics or Orthodox Jews. *Agostini* begins the process of leveling the political playing field.

Do the Requirements of Procedural Due Process and Equal Protection Apply to Litigation Arising Under the Establishment Clause?

Legally, the most significant aspect of *Agostini* is its reaffirmation of the evidentiary and remedial holdings in *Bowen v. Kendrick* (1988). In *Bowen*, the Court held that it was not enough for plaintiffs to prove that an organization is "religiously-inspired" or affiliated with a religious organization to make it ineligible to participate in public welfare programs. The proofs must also demonstrate that the government engaged in unconstitutional behavior.

The constitutional rule announced in *Aguilar*, by contrast, rested on speculation about matters impossible to prove. There was no actual misuse of public funds by the teachers employed by the New York City School Board, or any credible evidence they were "tempted" to engage in religious instruction. Justice Louis Powell, who cast the deciding vote in *Aguilar*, admitted as much when he noted that the educational programs involved "concededly have done so much good and little, if any, detectable harm."

Justice Powell voted to invalidate the programs anyway. In his view, "(the) State must be *certain*, given the Religion Clauses, that subsidized teachers do not inculcate religion."

This position raises two important questions:

1) What "adjudicative facts," if any, are relevant to a showing that government action violates the Establishment Clause?
2) How, as a practical matter, is such certainty to be achieved in any educational program or activity subsidized by the government?

A. The Relevance of Adjudicative Facts in Establishment Clause Litigation

Justice O'Connor's opinion for the majority in *Agostini* requires a showing that unconstitutional action is either imminent or in progress before federal or state aid to children enrolled in religious schools may be questioned on Establishment Clause grounds. The judicial role envisioned rests on a procedural due process model. Denial of the benefits under the statutory entitlement cannot take place until there is notice and an opportunity for the beneficiary to be heard, and proof that an illegal expenditure has been made.

Justice Souter's dissenting opinion takes a very different approach:

> I believe *Aguilar* was a correct and sensible decision, and my only reservation about its opinion is that the emphasis on the excessive entanglement produced by monitoring religious instructional content obscured those facts that independently called for the application of two central tenets of Establishment Clause jurisprudence. The State is forbidden to subsidize religion directly *and is just as surely forbidden to act in any way that could reasonably be viewed as religious endorsement.* (emphasis added)

Reduced to its essentials, the dissent's approach would permit no aid of any sort—including "remedial education even when it takes place off the religious premises"—to children enrolled in non-public schools. In Justice Souter's view, the "constitutional facts" that trigger a holding that the Establishment Clause has been violated are historical, political, and social, not adjudicative.

It has long been known that some factions in the political process will always perceive either an inability (or an unwillingness) on the part of subsidized teachers to comply with the "no religious content" rules the Court has developed. Among these are factions associated with "other religions that would like access to public money for their own worthy projects," factions who believe, on religious grounds, that religious groups should take no money from state funds, and advocates for a secular approach to publicly-funded education. We know, too, that some factions will always interpret direct or indirect payments made on behalf of children enrolled in schools having a religious perspective on education as an "endorsement" of the religion of the sponsoring organization. If the judgement is to rest on political and social grounds such as these, a trial is little more than constitutional window-dressing.

Justice O'Connor's approach requires a real trial, and proof that the government has actually done something wrong. More important, the majority opinion implicitly recognizes that "other religions" and groups having a secular ideological orientation already have access to substantial sums from the public fisc, and that they have used that access for years to support "their own worthy projects" (*e.g.* universities, hospitals, homes for the elderly, social welfare, adoption, and overseas relief agencies). History demonstrates convincingly that control of the rituals, curricula, and environments of the public schools has been the most "worthy" of all.

Agostini thus sets the stage for thorough reexamination of the constitutional and political legitimacy of the Court's approach to "The School Question."

B. The Establishment Clause and Judicial Affirmation of Structural Inequality
Agostini also paves the way for the reexamination of the structural inequality and religious intolerance evident in the Court's Establishment Clause decisions. The Court's assertion in Aguilar that "(the) State must be *certain*, given the Religion Clauses, that subsidized teachers do not inculcate religion" is a prime example of both. (emphasis added)

The five-Justice majority in Aguilar and the four dissenters in *Agostini* correctly observe that the only way to be *absolutely* certain that government subsidies for education will not be used for an improper purpose is to eliminate them. The position of these Justices, taken at face value, is that the need for prophylaxis is absolute. *All* education subsidies must be eliminated.

It seems clear, however, that these Justices do not mean what they say. Public schools have been inculcating a variety of state-approved religious beliefs and practices for nearly two centuries. Since at least the mid-nineteenth century, state officials have created and maintained public school environments hostile to the beliefs and practices of religiously-observant students who are adherents of religions holding minority status in their respective communities. In both word and deed, state-funded teachers have been inculcating state-approved messages concerning religion for years—and there is no indication from the reported cases that they have any incentive to stop.

Since there is *always a chance* that publicly-funded teachers will advance or inhibit religion in the course of their professional duties, consistent application of the Aguilar formulation would deny funding to both public and private schools. If publicly-funded teachers cannot express an opinion, either positive or negative, concerning religion, the members of the Court who support the reasoning in Aguilar have the guarantee that they believe the First Amendment requires. Parents, however, would not have access to any public funding for their children's education.

A "no-aid for education" approach would resolve a number of other thorny Establishment Clause issues too. Parents who want their children to have an education that includes an identifiable religious or moral perspective would bear the entire cost. The state could not prefer non-religion (secularism) over religion. No parent would have grounds on which to claim discrimination, and no observer, "reasonable" or otherwise, could possibly conclude that the government is supporting religious education.

It will not happen.

No Justice would even consider affirming an injunction against state expenditures for the support of children enrolled in public schools, even if a flagrant violation were to be found. When one considers that the ground asserted for the injunction in Aguilar was the chance that the activities of a teacher or administrator might violate the Establishment Clause, the disparity in treatment is clear. Schools having a religious perspective are held to a higher standard.

More serious is the reason for the disparate treatment. Four members of the Court in *Agostini* are hostile to any educational program that embodies a religious perspective on the subjects included in the curriculum. The bias, however, is "structural"; that is, it is deeply embedded in their cultural assumptions regarding the alleged "neutrality" of public schools.

Agostini does not entirely level the political playing field, however. It does set the stage for consideration of three key issues.

1. What are the substantive differences, if any, among elementary and secondary educational programs having "religious," "secular," and "non-sectarian" perspectives?
2. What are the criteria for distinguishing between and among educational programs that include such perspectives? and
3. What are the constitutional bases for arguments that the Constitution requires discrimination against educational programs that include "religious" perspectives.

Given the inherent vagueness of the constitutional definitions of the terms "religion" and "religious," as well as the paucity of scholarship on the meanings that should be attributed to the terms "secular" and "non-sectarian," it should be an interesting discussion.

Conclusion

Agostini is an important case, legally and politically. Its legal importance is simply stated. By requiring that opponents of aid to children enrolled in non-government schools produce evidence of unconstitutional behavior, the *Agostini* Court makes it feasible now to experiment with programs of public-private educational financing.

Viewed from a federalism perspective, *Agostini* stands for the proposition that the federal government (the Supreme Court) will not make a prophylactic rule that denies any possibility of aid to children enrolled in church-affiliated schools. It thus frees local political factions to bargain over the distribution of state and local money available for education.

And bargain they will. The public schools are under enormous political pressure to improve student achievement scores. They are under even greater fiscal and legal pressure to provide high-quality education at a reasonable cost. Litigation challenging the constitutionality of state education finance programs has been ongoing for twenty-five years. Several state supreme courts have ordered their respective legislatures to redesign the taxing and finance mechanisms used to support public schools. Billions of dollars are now in play, and the competition for scarce tax dollars has made the issue one of the most controversial in state and federal politics.

Federal rules prohibiting aid for children whose parents opt for education that does not occur in a state-controlled environment provide political "cover" for factions opposing aid to all children. They also make reasonable political solutions difficult to achieve.

If taxes are to be raised to support education reforms, it will be necessary to create broad-based coalitions that include all voters having an interest in the fair distribution of education funds. Voters who send their children to private and church-related schools pay taxes. So too do parents who homeschool their children. The increasing number of inner-city parents who have given up on the public schools' ability to serve the educational needs of their children have even longer-standing grievances.

Without the political support of these factions, compromise will be difficult. If they oppose proposed reforms because their children are shortchanged, compromise will be impossible.

Agostini also has significance for the ongoing debate in Congress over reform of the public welfare system. If the First Amendment forbids any "direct" payments to religious organizations because they might use the public welfare programs they administer as an opportunity to inculcate their religious views, many federal and state welfare reform proposals currently under consideration will never make it off the drawing boards.

In sum, *Agostini* affirms that there is a more rational, more egalitarian, and less political way to understand the liberties protected by the First Amendment. That such an approach will have a more egalitarian and less political impact on the distribution of public funds is also clear. Unfortunately, this is precisely what the dissenters fear.

Endnotes

1. Kenneth L. Karst, "Paths to Belonging: The Constitution and Cultural Identity," 64 *N. C. L. Review* 303, 340 (1986).

ON "DOCTRINE" AND THE ESTABLISHMENT CLAUSE

Michael Ariens

In an area of law known for its incoherence, what are we to make of Justice O'Connor's pronouncement in *Agostini* v. Felton that "our Establishment Clause law has 'significant[ly] change[d]' since we decided *Aguilar*." Is her statement defensible, or is *Agostini* just another example of the Court's Establishment Clause mood swings? If Establishment Clause jurisprudence has changed significantly since 1985, what caused that significant change? Does *Agostini* portend other changes in Establishment Clause jurisprudence?

Fifty years ago the Supreme Court began interpreting the meaning of the incorporated Establishment Clause. The Court's unanimous agreement in *Everson v. Board of Education* (1947) concerning the guiding principle of the "wall of separation" paled in light of the Court's 5–4 split concerning the application of the principle. In *Agostini*, the majority opinion for the Court, written by Justice O'Connor, notes that "the general principles we use to evaluate whether government aid violates the Establishment Clause have not changed since" 1985. Once again, despite this apparent unanimity regarding general principles, the Supreme Court's application of the general principles resulted not in unanimity, but another 5–4 decision.

This brief comment is intended to assess the possible horizon of *Agostini* in light of the Court's decades-long difficulty in reaching consensus in applying the reigning general principles of the Establishment Clause. Predicting the course of future Establishment Clause decisions by recourse to doctrine is a fool's game. Taking seriously Justice O'Connor's claim, however, may be profitable if only because Justice O'Connor is an extremely reliable barometer of the Court's Religion Clause decisions since *Aguilar*. (She has been with the majority in almost every Establishment and Free Exercise Clause case decided since *Aguilar*.)

The *Agostini* petitioners requested relief from the injunction issued in *Aguilar* on the grounds that *Aguilar* had been undermined in two ways; first, the call by five Justices in *Board of Education Kiryas Joel Village School District v. Grumet* (1994) to overrule *Aguilar*; and second, by three of the Court's intervening decisions. In *Witters v. Washington Department of Services for the Blind* (1986) the Court held that monetary assistance for vocational rehabilitation of the blind was constitutional even if it was used for religious vocational training. In *Zobrest v. Catalina Foothills School District* (1993) the Court held as constitutional a federal law which permitted a deaf student to bring his state-employed sign language translator to his religious high school. And in *Rosenberger v. Rector and Visitors of the University of Virginia* (1995) the Court determined that the University of Virginia Student Council's refusal to reimburse expenses incurred by a Christian student organization amounted to an unconstitutional viewpoint discrimination. The Court quickly rejected the first claim based on the *Kiryas Joel* decision. Although it accepted the second claim, it did so based solely on *Witters* and *Zobrest*. Justice O'Connor's opinion ignored *Rosenberger*.

Justice O'Connor claimed *Aguilar* and its companion case, *Grand Rapids v. Ball* (1985), rested on three assumptions: 1) a public employee working "on the premises of a religious school is presumed to inculcate religion in her work"; 2) the presence on religious school premises of persons employed by the public "creates a symbolic union between church and state"; and 3) public aid that directly assists the educational function of religiously-affiliated schools is impermissible even if the aid reaches such schools as a consequence of private decisions. Each of these premises, according to Justice O'Connor, has been undermined by the Court's Establishment Clause case law since 1985. The hunt, then, is for the cases that undermined those premises.

The first premise was not a presumption at all, but a rule of law. Unlike evidentiary presumptions, this presumption could not be rebutted. Once a court found that the public employee was engaged in work at a religious school, the presumption that the employee inculcated religion in her work followed as a matter of course. Such a rule, although massively over-inclusive, was believed necessary to avoid a symbolic link between religion and government. Justice O'Connor reads *Zobrest* as rejecting this presumption, and erecting a different presumption. Under *Zobrest*, courts must presume that the public employee "would dutifully discharge her responsibilities as a full-time public employee." It is unclear whether Justice O'Connor intends to use "presumption" in its evidentiary sense (that is, as rebuttable), or whether the *Zobrest*-presumption simply requires complainants to carry the burden of proof of religious inculcation. In either case, *Agostini* now requires a complainant affirmatively to prove that a public employee has inculcated religion while working at a religious school. This burden cannot be satisfied with allegations of improper behavior. So it is no longer possible to prevent the implementation of programs intended to benefit students attending religious schools by resort to the conclusive presumption of *Aguilar*. The fact-sensitive inquiry envisioned by the Court thus allows states to implement programs analogous to Shared Time and Title I programs, subject to a later court challenge if evidence exists that the public school employees are inculcating religion in their work.

"[W]e live by symbols," wrote Justice Frankfurter in *Minersville School District v. Gobitis* (1940). I do not doubt the truth of this claim, and I am confident that many Court watchers view the Court's decisions largely in symbolic terms. But the Court is not just creating symbols in its decisions; it is making a legal claim about some governmental program. To hold a program unconstitutional because it creates a symbolic union between government and religion requires both understanding whose symbolic reference chart the Court is adopting, and having a highly refined sense of how symbols are transmitted in a society of more than 250 million persons. Justice O'Connor mentions neither of these difficulties in her claim that *Zobrest* "implicitly repudiated [the] assumption . . . that the presence of a public employee on private school property creates an impermissible 'symbolic link' between government and religion." Instead, her claim is based on two assertions: 1) that there is no reason to assume a public employee will inculcate religion while working at the private school, and 2) that offering Title I services off-campus creates the same danger of a symbolic union as offering such programs on the premises of the religious school.

The first claim is a professionalism-based claim. A professional will be presumed to act ethically, and once one understands that a professional will act ethically, one should no longer fear the possibility of a symbolic union. This professionalism claim, if extended, permits a reexamination of *Lemon v. Kurtzman* (1971). In *Lemon*, one aspect of the Delaware law held unconstitutional was payment of salary supplements. Those supplements were limited to those teachers who taught subjects offered in the public schools, used teaching materials adopted in public schools, and who promised not to teach a course in religion while receiving a salary supplement. The *Lemon* Court acknowledged but minimized the professionalism argument:

> We need not and do not assume that teachers in parochial schools will be guilty of bad faith or any conscious design to evade the limitations imposed by the statute and the First Amendment. We simply recognize that a dedicated religious person, teaching in a school affiliated with his or her faith and operated to inculcate its tenets, will inevitably experience great difficulty in remaining religiously neutral.

It seems highly unlikely that *Agostini* implicitly calls for a reexamination of *Lemon*. Later in Justice O'Connor's opinion, the Court notes that the Title I program is a "carefully constrained program." Although such a prospect can be teased out of the majority's opinion, the Court expressly limits its opinion to constrained programs in which "private decisionmaking" and private decisionmakers are the only pathway between the governmental aid and the religious school.

The second claim is that the location of the Title I classroom makes no difference in terms of the "degree of symbolic union." Consequently, *Zobrest*, which permitted a publicly-paid translator to work at a religious high school, undermines *Aguilar*. What is left unsaid is whether the symbolic union rationale survives outside of this context. Will such reasoning still apply to cases allegedly involving religion in public schools, or to other instances in which it is claimed that religion is impermissible on public property?

The *Agostini* majority rejected the third premise of *Aguilar* and *Ball* by using the "child-benefit" theory, first enunciated in 1930 in *Cochran v. Louisiana State Board of Education*. The child-benefit theory distinguishes between aid given directly to religious schools, and aid given directly to children (or their parents), and only indirectly to those schools, as a result of the parents' private decisions. Although this theory has been controversial since *Everson v. Board of Education* (1947), the Court has never rejected it. Indeed, from the late 1960s through the 1970s, when the Supreme Court decided a number of cases involving aid to religious schools, the Court relied on the child benefit theory to justify holding some of these challenged programs constitutional despite the controversy attached to the theory. This precedent is one reason the *Agostini* majority's claim that *Witters* undermined this aspect of the rationale of *Aguilar* is unpersuasive. The opinions in *Witters* offer additional reasons.

In *Witters*, the Supreme Court held not violative of the Establishment Clause a Washington state program providing tuition assistance to handicapped students for vocational training, since the monetary assistance was paid directly to the student, who then determined whether to use this money at a religious or secular institution. There are several problems with the *Agostini* Court's use of *Witters*. First, the *Witters* Court noted that "[i]t is equally well-settled . . . that the State may not grant aid to a religious school, whether cash or in kind, where the effect of the aid is 'that of a direct subsidy to the religious school' from the State. . . . Aid may have that effect even though it takes the form of aid to students or parents." The citation for this proposition was *Grand Rapids v. Ball*. It seems rather difficult to suggest that Witters undermined *Aguilar* and Ball when the majority opinion in *Witters* cites *Ball* approvingly.

Second, immediately after noting that the Washington program was neutral as to religion, and thus consistent with Establishment Clause precedent, the Court continued: "Further, and importantly, nothing in the record indicates that, if petitioner succeeds, any significant portion of the aid expended under the Washington program as a whole will end up flowing to religious education." This condition suggests that there are significant limits on the use of neutral programs, even if the decisions "benefitting" religious schools are made as a result of private decisions.

Third, Justice O'Connor's concurring opinion in *Witters* cast doubt on the claim that *Witters* undermined the final premise of *Aguilar* and *Ball*. Her concurrence notes that "[a]s Justice Powell's separate opinion persuasively argues, the Court's opinion in *Mueller v. Allen* makes clear that 'state programs that are wholly neutral in offering educational assistance to a class defined without reference to religion do not violate the second part of the *Lemon v. Kurtzman* test, because any aid to religion results from the private decisions of beneficiaries.'" In *Mueller*, the Court held constitutional a Minnesota law permitting taxpayers to deduct the cost of educational expenses incurred in sending their children to any school. The vast majority of parents eligible for this deduction sent their children to religious schools, a fact pregnant with constitutional dimensions in the view of the *Mueller* dissenters (but irrelevant to the *Mueller* majority). Justice Marshall wrote both the dissenting opinion in *Mueller*, and the Court's opinion in *Witters*. His effort to condition neutral programs upon a showing that religious institutions were not unduly favored is an effort to refight *Mueller*, to limit it as much as possible to its facts. In contrast, Justice O'Connor, who joined the majority in *Mueller*, offers, in her *Witters* concurrence, a much broader interpretation of *Mueller*. *Mueller* was decided before *Aguilar* and *Ball*, and Justice O'Connor's concurrence in *Witters* suggests that it was *Mueller*, not *Witters*, that undermined *Aguilar*.

Fourth, the unanimity of the Court in *Witters* masked a deep division regarding the constitutionality of aid that might flow to religious schools. *Mueller*, *Aguilar*, and *Ball* were all 5–4 cases. During the time those cases were decided, membership in the Court remained the same. The only member of the Court to vote with the majority in each of these cases was Justice Lewis Powell. The thoroughgoing division of the other Justices suggests that *Witters* did not create new law; it was merely a rare case of the Court unanimously agreeing about a particular result.

Two other aspects of Justice O'Connor's opinion for the Court deserve mention. First, the Court holds that *Zobrest* also undermined *Aguilar*'s understanding of the excessive entanglement prong of *Lemon*. In the Court's opinion, the elimination of the presumption that public employees will inculcate religion, the presumption of pervasive monitoring of Title I teachers must also be abandoned. It would take a "far more onerous burden on religious institutions" than a program of monthly unannounced visits to reach an excessive entanglement.

Second, Justice O'Connor's opinion for the majority ignores *Rosenberger*. Why did Justice O'Connor note petitioners' reliance on *Rosenberger*, and then ignore it? Justice O'Connor's concurring opinion in *Rosenberger* noted that "[t]his case lies at the intersection of the principle of governmental neutrality and the prohibition on state funding of religious activities." Although she agreed that the program would not violate the Establishment Clause in this particular case, she concluded, "The Court's decision today therefore neither trumpets the supremacy of the neutrality principle nor signals the demise of the funding prohibition in Establishment Clause jurisprudence." I believe *Rosenberger* was not mentioned precisely because Justice O'Connor is not interested in abandoning the "funding prohibition." The avoidance of *Rosenberger* in *Agostini* strongly suggests that the change in Establishment Clause doctrine claimed in *Agostini* is slight. Until the Court determines to alter the foundation of Establishment Clause doctrine by reorganizing the "bedrock principles" of government neutrality and the prohibition on state funding of religious activities, it is premature to conclude that there has been a significant change in Establishment Clause doctrine.

Justice O'Connor's most lasting contribution to the interpretation of the Establishment Clause is the endorsement test (*Lynch v. Donnelly* (1984)). This test, which evaluates the constitutionality of governmental programs based on whether a reasonable observer would conclude that government had endorsed religion, offers her much room to maneuver about in deciding Establishment Clause cases. Further, her insistence on fact-specific inquiries allows Justice O'Connor great leeway to determine how to apply the neutrality of funding prohibition principles.

If by law we mean a principled judgment, there is no Supreme Court "law," or doctrine, when it comes to the Establishment Clause. *Agostini* fails to persuade me that we have entered an era in which doctrine will be clarified and understood. Although I agree with the Court's result in *Agostini*, its breadth of application and influence remains much in doubt, particularly because the Court is so sharply divided.

Justice O'Connor's *Agostini* opinion offers a wealth of possibilities to the interested legal academic. For that reason, the opinion should offer little comfort to those legislating and litigating in this field. Although much can be speculated about, little can be said with confidence. When Justice O'Connor joined the Court, those devoted to reading the Court's

Establishment Clause decisions knew that attempting to understand the Court's Establishment Clause doctrine required situating the views of Justice Powell. Since Justice Powell's retirement, observers of the Court have known that mapping the Court's Establishment Clause doctrine requires mapping Justice O'Connor's mind. For better and worse, *Agostini* confirms that the personal is the doctrinal.

Reading the Tea Leaves:
Agostini and Vouchers

Steven R. Shapiro

Many voucher proponents were quick to claim victory following last year's decision in *Agostini v. Felton* (1997). It is now preordained, they implied, that given the appropriate case the Supreme Court will uphold public funding for parochial school education through a system of tuition vouchers. Like the initial reports of Mark Twain's death, these proclamations are premature. Unlike Mark Twain's death, a Supreme Court decision upholding vouchers is far from inevitable. In fact, when *Agostini* is read carefully and in context, it points at least as strongly in the opposite direction.

At the outset, it is important to note that the fixation with *Agostini* is itself overstated. Thus far, voucher programs have been tested in four states and declared unconstitutional in each. All four cases were brought in state court. The decisions in Puerto Rico (*Associacion de Maestros de Puerto Rico v. Torres* [1994]) and Wisconsin (*Jackson v. Benson* [1997]) rested solely on state constitutional grounds. The decisions in Ohio (*Simmons-Harris v. Goff* [1997]) and Vermont (*Chittendon Town School District v. Vermont Department of Education* [1997]) relied on state and federal grounds. The United States Supreme Court may not, therefore, have the final word.

Contrary to Professor Viteritti's comments, elsewhere in this volume, I do not believe that a state constitutional ruling that strikes down a voucher plan would raise serious issues under either the federal Equal Protection or Free Exercise Clause. This is a Supreme Court, after all, that upheld, in *Harris v. McRae* (1980), the government's decision to fund childbirth but not abortion on the theory that the government need not pay for the exercise of constitutional rights. If that policy judgment is permissible, then surely the government can refrain from funding sectarian education so long as the secular education it offers is available to children of all faiths.

In any event, the free exercise claim is really little more than a restatement of the Establishment Clause problem, since a holding that vouchers violate the Establishment Clause would provide the compelling justification to defeat a free exercise claim. See *Lamb's Chapel v. Center Moriches School Union Free School District* (1993). We thus return to the first question: What does *Agostini* mean?

The broadest interpretation of *Agostini* is also the easiest to dismiss. *Agostini* plainly does not stand for the proposition that the only relevant question under the Establishment Clause is whether the government's funding decisions are based on religiously neutral criteria. Were that the case, the government could directly fund parochial schools themselves and justify the decision on the ground that government also funds public schools.

The Supreme Court's Establishment Clause jurisprudence may be confused, but it is certainly more nuanced than that. As Justice O'Connor said only two years earlier in *Rosenberger v. Rector and Visitors of the University of Virginia* (1995), "{t}he Court's decision today neither trumpets the supremacy of the neutrality principle nor signals the demise of the funding prohibition in Establishment Clause jurisprudence."

Indeed, Justice O'Connor's concurrence in *Rosenberger* is critical to understanding her majority opinion in *Agostini*. (Here, as in many other areas of the law, Justice O'Connor's views have disproportionate influence because she so often provides the essential fifth vote, as she did in both *Agostini* and *Rosenberger*.) Expressly disavowing any allegiance to a "Grand Unified Theory" of the Establishment Clause, she stressed the need to "focus on specific features of a particular government action to ensure that it does not violate the Constitution."

That is precisely how she approached the Establishment Clause question in *Agostini*, and the features of the Title I program on which she focused are revealing. First, the remedial services provided under Title I are designed to be supplementary, and thus do not relieve the parochial schools of costs they would otherwise have borne but for Title I funding, Second, the instructors in the Title I program are public school employees selected and supervised by the public school district. Third, there was no evidence in the record, and no common sense reason to believe, that public school teachers working in the Title I program would seize the opportunity to engage in religious indoctrination. Fourth, no public money from the Title I program ever goes "into the coffers" of the parochial schools.

None of these safeguards exist under any of the voucher schemes now being discussed. In contrast to Title I, vouchers provide unrestricted public funds that parochial schools may use for any and all purposes, including religious indoctrination. In contrast to Title I, vouchers are not limited to supplementary instruction; rather, they underwrite the basic operating costs of the parochial schools. And, in contrast to Title I, there is every reason to believe that the parochial school teachers funded through a government voucher program will inculcate religious values with the support of public money.

Ultimately, the critical question for Justice O'Connor is whether the use of public funds "to indoctrinate religion (can fairly) be attributed to the State." That is a complex inquiry, as anyone familiar with state action law knows. Despite the view of some voucher advocates, however, it is not as simple as asking whether the money goes to the parent or the parochial school. To the contrary, the Supreme Court has explicitly noted that state aid may be constitutionally impermissible "even though it takes the form of aid to students or parents." (*Witters v. Washington Dept. of Services for the Blind* (1986)).

Agostini's fact-based approach is consistent with the approach the Court has followed in other recent cases. For example, in *Rosenberger*, Justice O'Connor relied on three factors in concluding that the religious ideology of a student publication at the University of Virginia could not be "attributed" to the state although it was supported by student activity fees: the fees were distributed to a broad range of student publications, diminishing the likelihood that the school would be identified with the message of any particular one; the fees went to third party vendors and not to the publication itself; and dissenting students were entitled to a rebate on their contribution to the student fund.

In *Zobrest v. Catalina Foothills School District* (1993), the Court emphasized that the sign language interpreter that the state provided for the deaf parochial school student may have been transmitting a religious message but she was not formulating one. Thus, once again, the religious message could not be "attributed" to the state. In *Mueller v. Allen* (1983), there was no direct funding of any religious message. Instead, the state authorized a tax deduction for certain education expenses regardless of whether the child attended public or private schools. As a result, there was no money that passed from the public treasury to "the coffers of the parochial schools."

If anything, the most revealing aspect of *Agostini* for the current voucher debate may not be its treatment of *Aguilar v. Felton* (1985), which was overruled in its entirety, but its treatment of *Grand Rapids v. Ball* (1985), which was overruled only in part. The portion of *Ball* that was overruled was the portion that struck down a Shared Time Program that closely resembled Title I. The portion of *Ball* that was not overruled involved a Community Education Program that employed parochial school teachers to conduct community classes after school hours on parochial school grounds. Such programs remain unconstitutional even after *Agostini* precisely because they present a risk of publicly funded religious indoctrination that the Court found absent in Title I, but that is undeniably present when vouchers are used for parochial school tuition.

Finally, and perhaps most importantly, there is not a word in *Agostini* that casts any doubt on the Supreme Court's holding in *Committee for Public Education v. Nyquist* (1973), which is the closest the Court has ever come to reviewing a voucher program. New York in that case provided limited but unrestricted tuition reimbursement grants to parents of private school students. In striking down the program, the Court first noted that "these grants could not, consistently with the Establishment Clause, be given directly to the sectarian schools..." The Court then rejected the claim that the program was constitutional because the money went to the parents rather than the school. "Whether the grant is labeled a reimbursement, a reward, or a subsidy, its substantive impact is still the same."

The *Agostini* Court was certainly aware that its decision was being closely watched by those involved in the voucher debate. It gave no hint that *Nyquist* was in jeopardy. It did, however, caution the lower courts against concluding that "our more recent cases have, by implication, overruled an earlier precedent." Not even the strongest advocates of vouchers argue that they can be reconciled with *Nyquist*. After *Agostini*, the precedential weight of *Nyquist* has only been reinforced.

THE PLASTICITY OF POWER AND THE SUPREME COURT'S ESTABLISHMENT CLAUSE JURISPRUDENCE

Marci A. Hamilton

One often hears the lament that the Supreme Court's Establishment Clause jurisprudence is "all over the place," "inconsistent," and "a mess." The Court's decision in *Agostini v. Felton* (1997), which reverses a previously reached decision in the same case, is likely to be treated to similar criticism. The extreme criticism lodged against the Court's establishment doctrine, however, is undeserved. The critics of the Court's Establishment Clause jurisprudence have underestimated the deep importance of plasticity in the area and miscalculated the central values to be served by the Establishment Clause.

The Establishment Clause is one of the many structural features of the United States Constitution that is intended to divide power within the society. The Constitution partitions power between the federal branches, between the federal and state sovereigns, between these sovereigns and the people, and between church and state. The Convention's dominating, pragmatic method in framing the Constitution was to name the various sources of power in the society, to treat them as discrete centers, and then to determine, first, the kind and amount of power each entity should receive and, second, how to limit the power assigned. The goal was to achieve a balance within society in order to avoid the tyranny that springs from concentrations of social power. The Framers envisioned their project as the creation of a closed system of competing forces, much like—in the words of a delegate from Delaware, John Dickinson—a solar system. If the strands of power were kept separate, a balance was achieved, and the various power structures were pitted against each other. Thus liberty would be most secure.

The Establishment Clause, though added later, reflects this same concern. It was not enough to protect the free exercise of religion; it was also necessary to limit the power of religion so that it would not dominate the state. The

Constitution, taken as a whole, aims to achieve a pragmatic balance of power between church and state.

The Framers drafted a Constitution and James Madison drafted the First Amendment in "majestic generalities," rather than detailed concrete rules, because they were concerned at least in part about power's plasticity. Power, whether lodged in the church, the state, or the people, has a propulsive and corrupting quality. Social entities will strive to increase their power in ingenious and subtle ways and therefore there must be a great deal of flexibility in the system if the goal of a balance of power is to be achieved.

In *Agostini v. Felton*, the Court addressed the question whether the Establishment Clause is offended by public school teachers providing supplemental, remedial instruction on the premises of sectarian schools. The Court ruled that the teachers could teach on the premises of the sectarian schools.

Twelve years earlier, in *Aguilar v. Felton* (1985), the Court had held in the same case that the Establishment Clause prohibited public school teachers from entering the premises of sectarian schools.

The Court's reversal, led by Justice O'Connor, does not reveal intellectual or moral weakness, as some no doubt will charge.[1] Rather, it brings to the foreground the fact that the Court monitors its Establishment Clause jurisprudence for the purpose of assessing whether the appropriate balance of power has been achieved from the rules it has announced. In the *Aguilar-Agostini* story, the Court renders one decision on the grounds that any other scenario would result in an inappropriate balance of power and then reverses that decision in the same case after watching how the rule played out in practical terms. The result of the *Aguilar* rule defied common sense: in New York City alone, $10,000,000 each year was spent on trailers to be parked near the sectarian schools. If one takes the position that the Establishment Clause is intended to achieve a pragmatic balance of power between church and state, the first decision and the second decision are equally and validly warranted. The first was reached in good faith that its legal doctrine would produce the appropriate balance of power. The second was reached after practical experience had taught that the first decision was not warranted to preserve the balance of power between church and state.

Far from being castigated for reversing itself, the Court should be hailed for taking on the obviously unpopular role of demarcating the constitutional boundaries between interacting and changing social entities by gauging their factual relationship. The Court's monitoring of the pragmatic results of its establishment jurisprudence exhibits fealty to its constitutionally appointed role as interpreter of the Constitution in divining the boundaries of power between church and state. Such an attitude is absolutely essential if the Court is going to provide the sort of flexible guidance necessary in the face of power's plasticity.

The plasticity of social forces and the deceptively subtle way in which power can be exercised in the United States is illustrated by the simultaneous cultural belief that religion is marginalized in American politics and the contemporary political power of organized religion. In 1993, Professor Stephen Carter published the influential book, *The Culture of Disbelief: How American Law and Politics Trivialize Religious Devotion*, in which he argued that religion had become trivialized in American society. He claimed that there was "a trend in our political and legal cultures toward treating religious beliefs as arbitrary and unimportant, a trend that implies that there is something wrong with religious devotion." (Carter, p. 6) The book chronicled various concrete examples intended to prove that modern American culture forces religion and religious values to the margins. The *Culture of Disbelief* has had remarkable influence in many quarters, especially on Capitol Hill and in the White House.

The irony, of course, behind Professor Carter's book is that in the very year of its publication, organized religion, speaking through the Coalition for the Free Exercise of Religion, succeeded in persuading Congress to enact a law, the Religious Freedom Restoration Act (RFRA), which provided religion more leverage in church-state disputes than religion had ever had before. That law now placed the burden of proof on the government to justify its compelling need for any particular legislative action, and to demonstrate that this was the "least restrictive means" placed upon religion in order for the legislation to achieve its purpose, whenever any law unintentionally affected religious practice adversely. In short, religion could force government to defend itself whenever there was even inadvertant disadvantage to religion. Thus, the application of this two-part test to every generally applicable, neutral law signalled a sea change in the relationship between church and state.

Not only did religion receive a windfall at its behest with RFRA; it had succeeded in persuading Congress to play the role of religion's savior by overturning a Supreme Court decision, although this was plainly in derogation of the principle of separation of powers. The Coalition's aim had been for Congress to "fix" the Supreme Court's decision in *Employment Division v. Smith* (1990) and it delivered a draft bill that took the tack of overruling that decision. Thus, in achieving the Religious Freedom Restoration Act the Coalition not only attained its own goals, but also managed to prompt an unnecessary battle between two federal branches, a battle which it continues trying to exploit. This is the very play between power centers that the Framers assumed would take place and which prompted the various barriers on the exercise of power found in the Constitution.

The trick is to square Professor Carter's observations with these political realities, but it can be done. There is some force to his claim that a significant segment of society feels perfectly comfortable treating religion as nothing more than superstition. The question is the political impact of such anti-religion rhetoric. Is it necessarily bad for the fate of religion in politics? As Professor Carter notes, vast numbers of Americans believe in God and regularly pray. Thus, the rhetoric does not seem to have routed the religious sentiments of American citizens.

Perversely, the rhetoric of marginalization seems to have made it easier for religion to operate in Capitol Hill's backrooms. The Religious Freedom Restoration Act was not a product of the masses. Indeed, the average citizen knew nothing about it when it was passed and knows precious little now, after it has been invalidated (*Boerne v. Flores,* 1997). Rather, it was the product of Washington lobbyists for the various organized religions. They succeeded in spectacular style. The Religious Freedom Restoration Act was passed by a unanimous voice vote in the House and a near-unanimous vote in the Senate.

The rhetoric of marginalization cloaks religion's innate power, making it appear to be less strong than it actually is, and making it appear less threatening to entrenched power structures than it is. With the marginalizing rhetoric as its context, when religion complains about a Supreme Court precedent, it appears to need a protector. Congress, apparently, could not resist. It transgressed three constitutional structural boundaries in its rush to help religion: the separation of powers, federalism, and the Establishment Clause.

In this complex interplay of power, it should come as no surprise that the road to achieving the Establishment Clause's goal of a pragmatic balance of power is rocky at best. No one test can serve every circumstance and no one outcome may be appropriate for the ages, as *Agostini*'s overruling of *Aguilar* demonstrates. Instead, the Court, as an institution, has attempted to tailor its Establishment Clause jurisprudence to certain contexts, has monitored the practical effects of its rulings and has treated its cases as fact-specific. It has eschewed, in Justice O'Connor's words, "one grand unified theory." The complaint that this context-dependent, fact-dependent, and essentially humble approach lacks predictability casts a blind eye on the plastic quality of power and the ingenious ways in which church and state can achieve their goals. As one of the central players in the Constitution's construct, the Court seems to have grasped this essential postulate as it has labored to ensure a pragmatic balance of power between church and state.

Endnote

1. See Michael Ariens (this symposium) arguing that Justice O'Conner's position could only be explained as "personal."

AGOSTINI V. FELTON:
A 1997 RULING FOR THE AGES

Nathan Lewin

Serendipitously, *Agostini v. Felton*, decided on June 23, 1997, begins on page 1997 of the most recent Supreme Court Reporter. Is this an omen that the decision is good only for that year, and that supporters of school choice and parents of children attending religious schools will see no greater success in the future? Or does 1997—the historic case decided that year and reported on that page—mark a new beginning by the Supreme Court in the realm of public financing of secular programs provided in religious schools?

Agostini's good news is that five Justices of the current Supreme Court were ready—notwithstanding a significant procedural barrier—to eradicate a hurtful precedent that had, for more than a decade, irrationally deprived and hindered students in religious schools who need publicly financed remedial programs. *Agostini*'s bad news is that only five Justices agreed. Justices Souter and Breyer—who have expressed sympathy in the past, in one form or another, for the free exercise rights of believers—have now lined up with the strict separationists in the aid-to-private schools debate. Justice Souter's declaration, in his dissenting opinion, that "*Aguilar* was a correct and sensible decision" is most disheartening. By failing to join in Part I of Souter's dissent, Justice Breyer has, at least for the time being, withheld any personal approbation of *Aguilar*. But he agreed with Justice Souter's conclusion that, notwithstanding the cases decided by the Court since *Aguilar*, the 5–4 ruling issued in 1985 was still "good law" and should have been applied to the petitioners in *Agostini*. The fact that *Aguilar* was repudiated by only the thinnest of margins does not bode well for proponents of school choice.

Judges who have no hostile predilections against voucher programs should, however, find much in Justice O'Connor's majority opinion to uphold broad-based financial assistance programs for parents who are empowered to choose between public and private schools and to direct public funds accordingly. The Court majority unequivocally rejected the claim that is central to the constitutional challenge to voucher program, that "all government aid that directly aids the educational function of religious schools is invalid." And since elementary-school programs were involved in *Agostini*, the contention that government assistance is constitutionally permissible, under *Witters v. Washington Department of Services for the Blind* (1986), only to college-level education or higher is now dead and buried (unless, of course, a new five-member majority upends *Agostini*).

The characteristics of the Title I program involved in *Agostini* that were emphasized in Justice O'Connor's opinion are inherent in most voucher programs. First, the funds that a religious school realizes under a voucher program reach that school "only as a result of the genuinely independent and private choices" of the individual parents—a factor that was decisive in *Agostini*, as it had been both in *Witters* and in *Zobrest v. Catalina Foothills School District* (1993). It is not, therefore, government that is benefiting the religious school. It is, instead, the personal choice of a parent. The parallel provided by Justice O'Connor is on all fours with a voucher program. The benefit received by the religious school in *Agostini*, she said, is "no different from a State's issuing a paycheck to one of its employees, knowing that the employee would devote part or all of the check to a religious institution."

Second, the majority emphasized in *Agostini* that governmental assistance was "allocated on the basis of neutral, secular criteria that neither favor nor disfavor religion, and is made available to both religious and secular beneficiaries on a nondiscriminatory basis." When public financial assistance is provided to all eligible children, and no distinction is drawn between the religious and the secular, the law creates no "financial incentive" for religious indoctrination. It only prescribes a playing field that is level for the religious and the secular. The Constitution permits this flat terrain, even if private citizens choose religious education for their children rather than a secular private or public school.

Justice O'Connor's opinion does, however, meld some bad news with the good. *Lemon v. Kurtzman* (1978) may continue to spook the lower courts. (See Scalia, concurring in *Lambs Chapel v. Center Moriches Union Free School District* (1993).) And there are portions in the Agostini opinion that unfortunately distinguish for constitutional purposes between "supplementary" secular programs such as the remedial instruction in Agostini and the regular secular programs that are routinely provided by sectarian schools. Why governmental financing of an English literary history class is more dangerous to the separation of church and state than a government-financed class in remedial English is not immediately obvious—or even demonstrable after considerable thought. But Justice O'Connor's opinion makes this distinction.

In the voucher debate, as in so many Religious Clause issues that come before the current Court, the ultimate outcome with the Court as presently constituted depends on Justice O'Connor. And only God knows how she would rule, even in light of her stated views in *Agostini*.

STILL A LIMITED FREEDOM:
RELIGIOUS LIBERTY AFTER *AGOSTINI*

Joseph P. Viteritti

I have been asked to comment on the significance of the *Agostini* decision, or more specifically, how the ruling handed down by the United States Supreme Court in the spring of 1997 will affect the legal viability of school vouchers. Certainly, one is tempted to be cheerful, applauding the high Court's reversal of an unfortunate 1985 decision that prohibited public school teachers from providing federally supported remedial instruction to poor children on the premises of parochial schools. Clearly the five-person majority in the case intended to signal a deliberate philosophical change in direction from the strict separationist principles that dominated the Court in the 1970s, itself noting a more accomodationist approach to church-state relations that began to appear in earlier cases. The voucher issue, however, is far more complex.

Most constitutional scholars mark the turning point of Supreme Court jurisprudence with the Mueller decision of 1983, where it approved a tax credit that benefitted all parents regardless of where they sent their children to school. In this sense, *Aguilar* was an odd determination even for the mid-eighties. The pattern of greater accommodation was re-enforced by a series of rulings handed down later by the Rehnquist Court. In 1986, a unanimous Court in Witters declared that the First Amendment was not offended when a student used a public scholarship to attend a Bible college; in *Zobrest* (1993) the Court overruled the Ninth Circuit to uphold the right of a Catholic school student to receive the services of a sign language interpreter paid for with federal aid; in *Mergens* (1990) the Court found that public schools must permit student religious clubs to meet on campus under the same terms as other non-curricular organizations; in *Lamb's Chapel* (1993), it determined that Free Speech protections are violated when a public school denies the use of its facilities to a group wanting to show a film series with a religious perspective; and in *Rosenberger* (1995) the Court held that the University of Virginia could not discriminate against a student organization that wanted to use its activity fees to publish a newspaper with a religious viewpoint.

By permitting a public program to be administered on the premises of a religious institution, *Agostini* affirmed the accomodationist direction in which the Court had already begun to move, and this bodes well for advocates of school choice. More than a decade ago Justice Powell, in his concurring opinion in *Witters*, actually promulgated a set of principles for reviewing the constitutionality of state aid involving religious institutions. These standards, which still pertain, require that (1) aid is administered on a religiously neutral basis; (2) funds are equally available to those who attend public and private schools; (3) any aid to sectarian institutions is indirect, and the result of the private choices of individuals.

Opponents of school choice like to portray the last fifteen years of Supreme Court jurisprudence as an aberration from a well established constitutional tradition that imposes strict rules of separation under the Establishment Clause. Actually the opposite is true. The Framers themselves fully appreciated the distinction between disestablishment and separation, and understood a robust religious pluralism to be a foundation of democracy. As early as 1925 the Supreme Court, in *Pierce*, recognized the right of parents to determine the appropriate education for their children; and five years later, in *Cochran* the Court drew a significant legal distinction between aid provided to children and aid given directly to institutions.

All this seems to suggest—and *Agostini* supports the conclusion—that if the Supreme Court heard a voucher case today, it would find no conflict with the First Amendment so long as the conditions outlined by Justice Powell in *Witters* were met. But there are other obstacles to school choice inherent in *Witters* and not resolved by *Agostini* that may indeed be exacerbated by recent actions by the Court. *Witters* left the door open for an independent review of voucher plans by state judiciaries, based on provisions within their own state constitutions. Opponents of school choice have seized upon this opening to initiate litigation in the state courts. This explains why all the existing attempts to provide parents with choice through vouchers—in Wisconsin, Ohio and Vermont—are being contested before state judges.

In each of these three states, aid to parochial schools is indirect, purely a function of parental decisions to select a school in the best interests of their children. However, for reasons of administrative control, tuition checks are written both in the name of parents and of the schools that they choose. Voucher opponents have argued that this constitutes direct aid. Whether the Supreme Court agrees, and sacrifices the principle of parental choice on the alter of bureaucratic procedure remains to be seen.

The state constitutional issue is more complicated. Given the philosophical shift of the Supreme Court towards greater accommodation, voucher opponents are looking within the state documents for provisions that require more stringent standards of separation. The Rehnquist Court has been very sympathetic to state prerogatives in the way it defines federalism. The key constitutional issue for the federal court is whether strict standards of separation set by the states function in a way that violates the free exercise or equal protection rights of parents who would choose to send their children to religious schools. While the High Court has been sensitive to the issue of state authority, it has not hesitated to intervene in cases where it believes state power is used to abridge constitutionally protected rights, as it demonstrated in *Garcia* (1985), *U.S. Term Limits* (1995) and *Evans* (1996). For example, if a choice program adopted by a state specifically excludes religious institutions from participation, then there is reason to believe, based upon recent precedent, that the Supreme Court would reject such a plan.

However sympathetic the Supreme Court might be to the principles of parental choice and religious freedom, states have no legal obligation to provide support for parents who want to send their children to a private or parochial school. I know that the thought of treating school choice as an entitlement seems provocative to many people, but I raise it to make a point. Even most adamant opponents of school vouchers would agree that parents should be allowed to send their children to religious schools if they desire; they just don't want the costs paid for with state funds. What this means in a practical sense is that such choices are limited to those families who can afford it.

This financial responsibility can severely compromise the interests of deeply religious people who want to see their children educated according to the principles of their faith, or whose religious convictions are undermined in value-laden public school curricula that are implemented in the name of secularism. Such costs impose a serious burden on the practice of one's faith. I recall, for example, a situation in New York City several years ago where all public school children were required to enroll in a sex education program, even if its message and teachings were in direct conflict with their religious beliefs. In a more recent instance, Jewish children were required by an Alabama school board to remove their yarmulkes and recite a Christian prayer.

Of course in both the latter cases, the families had options. They could initiate legal proceedings against the school board, or leave the public school for a private institution that was not antagonistic to their beliefs. Either way they would be expected to assume the expenses of their actions, while continuing to pay taxes to support the public program that offended them. If they could not bear the costs, then they had no choice but to stay put and do what they were told.

Agostini notwithstanding, so long as the opportunity for parents to select a school that honors the dictates of their conscience is conditioned by economics, religious liberty in America is a limited freedom.

Equality, Not Preference or Discrimination

Eugene M. Volokh

Does the Constitution require discrimination against religious schools? This question is the heart of the Establishment Clause debate over school choice. May the government treat public schools, secular private schools, and religious schools equally, paying for children's education regardless of the religiosity of the school to which the children go? Or must the government exclude religious schools from this generally available benefit?

The right answer, I think—for Jews as well as for all others—is that the Constitution demands equality, not preference or discrimination. The government must treat everyone equally, without regard to religiosity. It must not prefer either a particular religion, or religion generally. But neither must it discriminate against religious people and religious institutions.

The U.S. Supreme Court's precedents are in tension on this: In the 1970s, liberal Supreme Court majorities, often led by Justices Brennan and Marshall, seemed to suggest that the Constitution does require discrimination against religion, but the 1980s and 1990s saw a slow retreat from this position and towards a neutrality model.

Curiously, though, the neutrality model flows from egalitarian principles that are firmly rooted in liberal traditions. Justice Brennan himself captured this view well when he said—in striking down a law that banned clergy from public office (*McDaniel v. Paty*, (1978))—that "government may not use religion as a basis of classification for the imposition of duties, penalties, privileges or benefits."

Such "discriminat[ion] between religion and nonreligion," Brennan (joined by Marshall) wrote, "manifests patent hostility toward, not neutrality respecting, religion." "The Establishment Clause does not license government to treat religion and those who teach or practice it, simply by virtue of their status as such, as subversive of American ideals and therefore subject to unique disabilities." The Constitution, if this view is taken seriously, requires equal treatment of religion, not discrimination against it, in fact, we usually take this neutrality principle for granted, consider police protection, fire protection, garbage collection, the GI Bill, and many other programs. We would be appalled if the police and fire departments refused to take calls from churches and synagogues, on the theory that "there's a wall of separation around your temple, and we can't cross it to help you. Hire your own separate firefighters and security guards." We expect the government to give no preference to religious institutions, but we wouldn't tolerate the government discriminating against them, either.

This widely agreed-on conclusion suggests that "separation of church and state" need not equal "no support given by the state to churches." Rather, separation must mean "no special support given by the state to churches *because they are churches*." The state could separate itself from questions of religion by treating people and institutions equally without regard to their religiosity. A legislator's or 911 caller's religiosity would, under this view, be of no concern to the state.

Once this neutrality principle is accepted as to some services, it's hard to reject for K–12 education, one of the most valuable services that the modern welfare state provides. Why must religion, which may be treated equally in other areas, be discriminated against here? Why not separate government from religion by having it evenhandedly support parents' educational choices, without getting the state involved in examining whether the education is religious?

The responses of Establishment Clause critics of school choice fall into five main categories.

Aid to Religion School choice programs, critics say, help religious schools and thus aid propagation of religion. This is true, but it can't distinguish education from other neutrally available services: Religion is aided when the government protects religious schools against crime, picks up their trash, or gives them neutrally available disaster relief assistance. These programs are constitutional because they help everyone, religious or not; the principle must be that equal treatment is not "establishment." How is school choice funding different?

Well, critics continue, this is your and my tax money—not just government services—indirectly flowing to religious teaching. "Taxpayers will be coerced into supporting religions, including sects and cults, with which they may not agree," says an ACLU news bulletin condemning a neutral school choice plan. Shocking!—or is it?

Tax money indirectly flows to religion all the time, with no constitutional impropriety. I, as a University of California employee, might donate part of my paycheck to a synagogue, or even, horror of horrors, a sect or a cult. Many welfare or social security recipients donate parts of their incomes to a church. (Some churches and religious schools, for instance ones near military bases or ones whose congregations are poor and elderly, may be supported almost entirely by contributions that indirectly come from government coffers.) A blind student may choose to use state vocational education funds to train for the ministry, something the U.S. Supreme Court unanimously upheld in the *Witters* case (1986). College students can spend GI Bill funds or Pell grants or student loans majoring in theology at Yeshiva University as well as in math at UCLA.

If these private choices are permissible—as most agree they are—then it can't matter whether tax money ends up in church hands: What must matter is how the money gets there. If people individually decide to route their tax-supported paychecks, welfare checks, or scholarships to religious institutions, there's no Establishment Clause violation. And this is exactly what happens under religiously neutral school choice programs, which are GI Bills for children. As in the examples given above, any funds that flow to religious schools go as a result of the parent's private, uncoerced decision.

Pervasive Religiosity Ah, some say, religious K–12 education is different because it's "pervasively religious." But many colleges are pervasively religious, too; *Witters*, recall, was studying to be a minister. Donations by government aid recipients to churches also go to pervasively religious uses. We accept that returning GIs or blind people or Pell grant recipients may use their government-supplied funds to teach themselves religiously—it's hard to see constitutional difficulty in their using similar funds to teach their children religiously.

Effects Well, some argue, maybe school choice programs look neutral, but in effect they really aren't, because most of their funds end up being spent at religious schools. But this is like claiming that putting out a fire at a church is unconstitutional because the firefighters are primarily helping the church. Looking at education or firefighting as a whole, we see the bulk of the money goes to nonreligious institutions—90 percent of all schools throughout the country are secular, either government-run or private.

Under school choice, the money goes to all schools instead of only to government-run ones. To follow the fire analogy, it's as if the government used to exclude private schools from fire protection, but recently switched to a more evenhanded approach. This expansion to a more inclusive framework, a framework that treats religious institutions the same way it treats others, isn't a preference for religion.

Quid Pro Quo Could discrimination against religion be a sort of compensation for religious institutions' tax exemption? Actually, property tax exemptions, as well as charitable exemptions from income taxes, fit the neutrality mold: They are generally upheld precisely because they apply to all charitable institutions, whether religious or not. (A 1989 Supreme Court case in fact struck down, on neutrality grounds, a special tax exemption for religious publications.) Private nonprofit secular schools are just as tax-exempt as private nonprofit religious schools. And parents who send their kids to private religious schools pay taxes just like parents who send their kids to secular schools.

Original Intent A decision upholding a religiously neutral school choice system, the president of People for the American Way opined, would set "Thomas Jefferson and James Madison spinning in their graves." Wasn't the Establishment Clause originally intended to prevent any government funds from flowing, even indirectly, to religious institutions? Well, no.

The Framers' criticisms of religious establishment were leveled at preferential aid to religion, not at neutral individual choice programs. For instance, James Madison's *Remonstrance Against Religious Assessments* (1786)—often cited by school choice critics—was actually aimed at a preference scheme called the "Bill Establishing a Provision for Teachers of the Christian Religion," which Madison said "violate[d] that equality which ought to be the basis of every law."

The relatively minimal late-1700s governments gave the Framers no occasion to think about government funds indirectly flowing, through private choices under genuinely evenhanded benefit programs, to religious institutions. And I'm aware of no evidence that the Framers meant to enshrine discrimination against religion as a constitutional command.

Harm to Religion Would government funds inevitably bring government oversight and regulation, thus compromising religious schools' independence? Could school choice be unconstitutional because it's bad for religion?

This is a reasonable concern, but the government already has broad authority to regulate private schools, including religious ones. State governments can (and often do) require that all schools comply with health, safety, and antidiscrimination laws, obey minimum curriculum requirements, hire only certified teachers, and so on.

Some conditions—such as a requirement that schools honor parents' requests to excuse their children from religious activity—are indeed made possible by the funding. But it's hard to see how the ban on establishment of religion prohibits religious schools from voluntarily accepting such strings. True, the offered funding might pressure schools into accepting this condition, but if we care about such pressure, we should also consider the pressure created by the non-school-choice regime: Millions of parents are similarly pressured by the offer of free government-run education into sending their kids to government-run schools, even when they'd otherwise prefer a religious education. School choice should in the aggregate diminish this secularizing pressure; and it should increase the options available both to parents and to religious schools.

If this argument is correct, then neutrality is at least constitutionally allowed. I'd go further and argue that neutrality is constitutionally compelled: that the government may not discriminatorily exclude religious schools from school choice programs. The *McDaniel* case supports this view; so does the more recent *Lukumi Babalu Aye* (1993) case, which held that the government may not treat religiously motivated practices (there animal sacrifice) worse than identical secular practices.

Likewise, the Court's Free Speech Clause cases suggest the government may not discriminate against private religious teaching and in favor of private secular teaching, even when the discrimination involves distribution of money. The claim isn't that the government *must* fund school choice: It may still fund only government-run schools and not private ones, because such a distinction would be based on government control, not religiosity. Rather, the claim is that any choice programs that help secular private schools may not exclude religious private schools.

This, though, is a tougher battle, at least today, and one the school choice forces are only starting to fight. Right now, they focus mostly on defending neutrality as a *permissible* option—on persuading courts that the Constitution doesn't require discrimination against religion.

And this, I think, must be the right result. The Constitution bars the "establishment of religion," and treating everyone the same without regard to religion is hard to see as "establishing" anything—except equality.

Section Three:
Implications of a School Voucher Program for the Jewish Community

INTRODUCTION

David M. Gordis

Our discussion now moves from the historical, legal, and general public policy dimensions, to specific Jewish communal considerations. As in the earlier stages of discussion, the issues are complex, embracing philosophical, social-ethical and pragmatic concerns.

The commentators on these particularly Jewish issues are unanimous on the centrality of Jewish education, especially day school education, to the public agenda of American Judaism. Anxiety over Jewish continuity, which reaches across the denominational and ideological board, translates into the need to expand resources for Jewish education. Our contributors consider the day school as a central instrument to reinforce Jewish identity, but point to the massive economic challenge faced by the community in finding resources to make day school education available, if not to all, then at least to far larger numbers of children than receive such education today. Whether school vouchers can help alleviate the problem remains an open question. Predominant opinion in the Jewish community is still opposed to the approach, citing problems of quality control and of interference in school governance which would be an inevitable result of public aid. There is also concern about potential damage to the public school system, which is still viewed as an effective tool for building intergroup relations in this country. On the other hand, there are some supporters of school vouchers who regard those views as the obsolete and self-destructive position of "liberals" and "secularists," whom they hold responsible for every social and ethical pathology plaguing society. Intermediate positions support more modest experiments to evaluate small-scale voucher programs as well as other models of school choice, such as magnet schools and specialized schools, along with greater investment in upgrading public schools.

Both advocates and opponents of vouchers are aware that any support for day schools that a voucher program might provide would only marginally touch the economic challenges the community faces in funding day schools.

There are certainly borderline cases where voucher funds would make the difference between affording and not affording a day school, but those cases are likely to be few in number. For the most part, the challenge of funding day schools will have to be met through large scale Federation and private philanthropic initiatives such as those described here.

It should be noted that Jewish voucher advocates sometimes explain their position in terms of the need to confront the catastrophic problems of inner-city schools. Their view is that even if a voucher plan is adopted, it may well be targeted specifically to those schools. In any event, it would hardly make a dent in Jewish day school funding needs. Their support of vouchers, then, is not an exercise in self-interest, but an expression of the traditional Jewish objective of Tikkun Olam, "repairing the world." This should convince even the more ideologically inclined among us that constructive deliberation about vouchers need not descend into political and ideological wrangling. To succeed in that would be quite an achievement in Jewish public policy deliberation.

The Jewish Experience in American Public and Private Education

Jonathan D. Sarna

I am grateful to the conference organizers for the very modest task they have assigned to me. I have 343 years to cover in about 20 minutes. That leaves me about 3.5 seconds a year, so I may leave one or two things out. Permit me, then, at the outset (and without all the attendant footnotes) to make three points about the history of Jews and American education that I think are relevant to our deliberations here.

First, it is critically important to recognize that the history of American-Jewish attitudes concerning the role of religion in the schools (and indeed, concerning religion-state issues generally) is both more complex and more variegated than generally recognized. There is no monolithic Jewish view on this subject, and the community's attitudes have changed markedly over time, as historical conditions have changed.

Second, we can point to at least two principles that the Jewish community has broadly accepted over the centuries. The first is the principle of "equal footing"—the idea that all faiths, large and small, should be treated equally. There should be no special privileges for being a Protestant or a Catholic. And the second principle is that the public schools should be non-sectarian. At the very least, they should not be engaged in covert missionizing. I think that on those two points there was, and remains, a very broad Jewish communal consensus.

The third point is that a fundamental change has taken place since the 1960s in American-Jewish attitudes toward public schooling, reflected in the astounding and continuing growth of Jewish day-schools. This new situation—the fact that today about 28 percent of Jewish children who receive any form of Jewish religious education receive it in the day-schools—sets the stage for the kinds of policy changes that we will be considering here.

(Let me explain why Jews use the word "day-school." For all intents and purposes these are parochial schools, but the term "parochial" comes from a word meaning "diocese" or "parish," and implies that the school was established and maintained by a religious body. Since the Jewish schools are generally independent or congregationally-sponsored entities, the term "day-school" has become normative.)

So much for conclusions and definitions. Now, let me turn to some history. Early 19th century Americans, Jews and Christians alike, assumed that religion and education were closely intertwined. Congress gave legal expression to that idea in the Northwest Ordinance of 1787, declaring in its second article that "religion, morality and knowledge being necessary to good government and the happiness of mankind, schools and the means of education shall forever be encouraged." In New York City, where some 400 Jews resided in the early nineteenth century, almost all schools were religious in character. There was plenty of school choice back then. There were the "common pay" (or private) schools, which generally assumed the religious identity of the headmaster. The "charity" or "free schools" were supported by the city's churches and could draw upon the state's School Fund. And the Jewish community was part of this. In 1803, New York's only Jewish congregation, Shearith Israel (which is known today as the Spanish and Portuguese Synagogue), established a charity school under its own auspices named Polonies Talmud Torah. The school enjoyed equal footing with the Protestant and the Catholic schools in the city, and received state aid.

In 1813, in response to a challenge from the nondenominational New York Free School (the forerunner of the Public School Society), which wanted all state money to flow to its schools, Shearith Israel, in concert with Presbyterian, Baptist, Methodist and Catholic churches, sent a petition to the New York legislature, defending state aid to religious schools. That petition reflects what Shearith Israel's Jews thought was best for their children, their community, and their country as a whole, and it is fascinating for us now because it expresses views that are diametrically opposite to those that we generally associate with American Jews, views that would only emerge a few decades later. So, for example, the congregation's leaders condemned the New York Free School in this petition for raising children "unacquainted with the principles of any religion." We "conceive religion the greatest foundation of social happiness—the best pledge of republican institutions—and the greatest security of property, of liberty and of life," they wrote. They charged that the effort to restrict state funds to the free school alone was "at variance with the liberal spirit of our Constitution, which recognizes no distinction in public worship." It was a very persuasive petition and it was successful. Religiously sponsored charity schools, including Shearith Israel's, continued to receive state assistance until 1825.

Ultimately, of course, the idea of the free, nondenominational public school triumphed in New York and throughout the country. Initially, however, Jews who could afford to do so actually avoided these kinds of schools because they were really culturally Protestant. Their curriculum and textbooks were rife with material that Jews (as well, by the way, as Catholics) found profoundly offensive. As a result, Jews, when they could, sent their children to Jewish schools, which flourished not only in New York, but in every major city where Jews lived.

Public schools, however, had a great advantage, especially to new immigrants, because they were free, and often were superior in quality. As they became more religiously sensitive (that is, de-Protestantized), Jews flocked to them. This engendered considerable debate during the middle of the 19th century. In 1855, for example, a St. Louis man named Isadore Busch wrote a ringing endorsement of the public school, which he described as a "grand institution." He declared himself "utterly opposed to all sectional or sectarian schools"—meaning Jewish day schools—on pragmatic, economic and ideological grounds: pragmatic, in that most Jewish children would not attend them; economic, in that most Jews could not afford them; and ideological, in that public schools are an important instrument of Americanization. Jews should be grateful, he argued, that there was such an institution as public schools, and should support them. In a sense, he reversed the Shearith Israel argument, maintaining that the public schools were better for children, better for the Jewish community, and better for the nation at large. He advocated that the Jewish community use supplementary schools for religious instruction. In other words, public schools for secular education, and afternoon and Sunday schools for religious education.

There was considerable opposition to Busch's argument at the time. Isaac Leeser, the editor of the journal, *The Occident*, where Busch's letter appeared, and actually a founder of the Sunday school system in Philadelphia, nevertheless disagreed with Busch. "Mr. Busch," he wrote, "overrates the advantages of a public school education and underrates the difficulties of evening religious schools." Although an organizer of a Sunday school system, Leeser continued to support Jewish day schools as the ideal.

That debate is revealing, but I suppose it's even more revealing that ultimately the Busch position won the day. By the middle of the 1870s, most of the Jewish day-schools had closed, replaced by Sabbath, Sunday, and afternoon supplementary schools. "It is our settled opinion here," Rabbi Isaac Mayer Wise, the great Cincinnati Reform Jewish leader, reported to the U.S. Commissioner of Education in 1870, "that the education of the young is the business of the state, and that religious instruction . . . is the duty of religious bodies. Neither ought to interfere with the other."

That settled opinion was to become ideology. To attend public schools, and to guard them from sectarianism, became not just a matter of Jewish communal interest but, as Jews saw it, actually a patriotic obligation as well. Indeed, Jews came to look upon the public schools as symbols of American democracy. "Temples of liberty," one Cincinnati Jewish leader called them, where "children of the high and low, rich and poor, Protestants, Catholics and Jews mingle together, play together and are taught that we are a free people, striving to elevate mankind, and to respect one another." As such, the public schools came to have an insurmountable advantage over sectarian schools. From the late 19th century, Jews perceived them as an entree to America itself and supported them as nothing less than a patriotic duty. Thus, while the Catholic Church looked upon the public school as a symbol of much that was wrong with America, and therefore set up its own system of parochial school education, Jews wholeheartedly supported and even idealized public education as a symbol of America's promise.

Still, Jews did understand that there remained a considerable gap between promise and reality in many of those public schools that Jews actually attended, particularly with respect to the role of religion. Numerous schools, for example, began their day with morning religious exercises of a very Protestant nature, which hardly accorded with the American ideals that Jews thought the public schools were supposed to inculcate. The question which agitated the American-Jewish community for the better part of a century was how to oppose sectarianism in the schools without embracing total secularism. Jewish leaders were by no means of one mind on that issue. Some, like Rabbi Isaac Mayer Wise, believed that religious education should be the exclusive responsibility of parents and clergymen. Others, like the great liberal rabbi of the nineteenth century, Rabbi Bernhard Felsenthal, called for schools to teach what he called "unsectarian ethics"—a whole graded curriculum, embracing such concepts as "virtue and vice, equanimity and passion, good and evil, true and untrue, egoism and altruism," which he thought would be acceptable in the public school setting. Still others, like the more traditional Jews who edited the journal *The American Hebrew*, believed that schools might teach "the three great religious facts upon the verity of which all religions are united." Those were, to their mind, the existence of God, the responsibility of man to his Maker, and the immortality of the soul.

A particularly interesting intra-Jewish debate surrounded the so-called Gary Plan—in some ways analogous to our discussion here today. The Gary Plan, initiated in Gary, Indiana in 1913, permitted released time during the school day for moral and religious instruction outside of school property. Many rabbis opposed the plan, in spite of its nationwide popularity, fearing that once the wall between church and state was breached, "the religion of the majority will receive general sanction." But there were other rabbis who viewed this idea very positively, particularly the version known as "dismissed time," where the school day would end early to allow students to attend religious schools. "We have a unique and therefore very delicate problem," explained New York's Rabbi Samuel Schulman, a leading Reform rabbi. "We, of course, want to keep religion, Bible reading, hymn singing, out of the public schools. At the same time, we know that there is not enough efficient moral and religious education in the country." He called upon American Jews to "constructively and helpfully meet all efforts made for the improvement of ethical and religious education in the nation." The Jewish community was so divided on this issue that in one memorable case early in the 1940s, the Northern California Board of Rabbis opposed a released time bill, while the Southern California Board of Rabbis supported it.

Once the Supreme Court outlawed many forms of released time in the *McCollum* case (1948), these divisions healed. It was at this point in time, after World War II and with the move from state to national consideration of school issues (thanks to the 1940 Supreme Court decision in the *Cantwell* case), that we see a much broader separationist consensus emerge within the American Jewish community, symbolized by the establishment of the "Joint Committee on Religion and the Public Schools" (later known as "the Joint Committee on Religion and State"). The committee represented the full spectrum of Jewish religious and communal life, from anti-religious to Orthodox, including Conservative and Reform, all of them supporting a high wall of separation between church and state. In the wake of the school prayer and Bible reading cases of the early 1960s (*Engel v. Vitale, Abington v. Schempp*, etc.), this Jewish consensus seemed totally in harmony with the position of the U.S. Supreme Court. As a result, only a small number of voices in the community sounded notes of discord. (The most famous dissenter, as my friend Professor David Dalin has shown, was Will Herberg.) Most Americans rejoiced that religion was now out of the schools completely.

It was at this point that attention largely shifted away from the issue of religion in the public schools—Jews thought that was more or less settled—and toward the question of state aid to parochial schools. Unlike school prayer, the issue here did not involve the question of Jewish equality, or "equal footing." The aid was offered to Christian and Jewish schools alike. Instead, it revolved around the "wall of separation" axiom upon which Jews constructed so much of their twentieth century church-state philosophy. The debate, which began in earnest in the 1960s, pitted advocates of principle, who felt that any breach in the wall of separation would affect America and its Jews adversely, against proponents of pragmatism, who argued for an accommodationist policy benefiting Jewish day schools, interfaith relations, and American education as a whole. The voucher issue that we are discussing today is in many respects a continuation of this debate from the 1960s.

As we have already seen, historically, before the modern public school system existed, Jews readily supported state aid to parochial schools, and in fact Shearith Israel received such aid. But subsequently, the issue scarcely ever arose in Jewish circles, partly because Jews held public schooling in such high esteem, and partly because Jews and Protestants did not, by and large, view Catholic parochial schooling with any esteem at all. They looked upon it, indeed, with a great deal of suspicion. As late as 1927, there were no more than twelve Jewish parochial schools in the whole United States. What changed all of this was, first, the growth of Jewish day-schools in the post-war period, and especially from the late 1950s, first Orthodox, then non-Orthodox; second, the increasing concern over public education, particularly in the wake of the Cold War, and Russia's success in launching the Sputnik satellite, and later the effects of court-mandated changes in public education (such as the end of school prayer, racial bussing, and curricular changes); and third, heightened Catholic pressure to alleviate what they understandably perceived as an unfair burden upon them of essentially paying twice for their children's education. These and other factors led to a reexamination of the consensus Jewish view on state aid to parochial schools, particularly (although not exclusively) on the part of the Orthodox community, who not coincidentally were also the strongest proponents of Jewish day schools. In 1962, the *American Jewish Yearbook* noticed for the first time what it described as "unexpectedly strong support for the Catholic position," favoring state aid to parochial schools, that had "appeared within the Jewish community, especially among the Orthodox." In 1965, when Congress debated the Elementary and Secondary Education Act that included "child benefit" money earmarked for special educational services to parochial and private schools, intra-Jewish divisions came out into the open, and Jewish spokesmen testified before Congress on both sides of the issue, something that had not happened on a church-state question since World War II.

Since then, and quite literally to this very day here in Washington, the Jewish community has consistently spoken with two voices whenever proposals like the voucher system are put forward. Each side musters support from the past. Each side, as we have now seen, can legitimate its position historically. But in the final analysis the central question is not basically an historical one. It is really a pragmatic one. Quite simply, what do we think is best for our children, for our community, and for our country? That was the question that underlay the petition of Shearith Israel's Jews back in 1813. It was the question that Isadore Busch answered, quite differently, in 1855. And it remains the central question that we need to address here today.

THE CASE OF THE JEWISH DAY SCHOOL

Alvin I. Schiff

Emergence and Growth of the Day School

One of the most exciting and meaningful phenomena in the American Jewish community in the twentieth century has been the development and growth of Jewish all-day education. In the first half of this century the American Jewish community was wedded to the idea of the public school. The avid support of public education by virtually all Jewish immigrants in the late 1800s and early 1900s derived from their perception of the public school as the gateway to Americanization. They saw in public education the fulfillment of their dreams—being accepted in the larger society and being given the opportunity to advance intellectually, professionally and economically as equals with the gentile population.

Jews desiring to maintain the Jewishness of their public school children organized Jewish educational programs after school hours and on Saturdays and Sundays. These could take the form of private tutelage held in the homes of either the pupils or the teachers; or a small, one room and one teacher school (*heder*); or a Sunday school or community Hebrew school (*Talmud Torah*). Privately tutored pupils and children studying in the heder or Sunday school received one or two hours of Judaic instruction weekly. Students in the Talmud Torah generally studied Jewish subjects several afternoons and Sunday mornings for a total of 8 to 10 hours per week.

The private tutor, the *heder* and the *Talmud Torah* were gradually replaced by the supplementary congregational school, sponsored by Conservative and Orthodox synagogues. By the end of the 1930s the congregational school, where pupils studied from 4–6 hours per week, had become the primary institution of Jewish instruction for children and youth in Conservative and Orthodox synagogues. The curriculum of the synagogue school consisted of Hebrew language (phonics and basic comprehension), *Siddur*, (mechanical prayer book reading in Hebrew), Bible stories in English or in simple Hebrew, Jewish holidays, customs and ceremonies, Jewish history and Jewish current events. The Reform movement adopted the Sunday School idea (two hours a week), stressing Judaic study in the English language. Over the years, many Reform temples added one or two elective weekday afternoons for Hebraic programs.

Congregational schooling, particularly under Conservative and Reform auspices, grew rapidly in the 1930s and 1940s, and flourished for almost two decades after World War II as synagogues thrived and expanded in membership and facilities. By 1962, the peak year of Jewish school enrollment in North America, there were some 540,000 pupils in congregational schools in the United States and Canada. Since then, the congregational school has been on the decline. Thirty five years later there are only 270,000 pupils enrolled in these schools—a decrease of fifty percent—due largely to a diminishing birthrate, to an increase in intermarriage, and to the acculturation pattern of young endogamously married Jewish couples who do not feel the need to provide Jewish education to their progeny. Family breakup and the adverse attitudes of many Jewish parents to their own Jewish supplementary educational experience have also affected negatively the enrollment in Jewish religious schools. In addition, funding and transportation issues have impacted upon Jewish supplementary education.

Moreover, recent studies of Jewish supplementary schooling demonstrate that this form of Jewish education has become, by and large, incapable of achieving its goals. Among the reasons for the current ineffectiveness of Jewish supplementary education are the low priority status of the school and of life-long learning within the synagogue; the lack of home support; and the shortage of adequately trained supervisory and instructional personnel.

In contrast to the downward trend of the Jewish supplementary school, the Jewish day school has enjoyed remarkable growth—from 60,000 pupils in 280 schools in North American in 1962 to 182,000 in 660 schools in 1992. Estimates of the 1996–1997 enrollment in Jewish all day educational institutions from pre-school through post high school programs reach 200,000. The Jewish day school population represented about 40 percent of the total North American Jewish school enrollment in 1996 and about 20 percent of the total Jewish population of school age. In 1996, about 10 percent of the Jewish population between 20 and 40 years of age had attended Jewish day schools through grades 6, 8 or 12.

Today's Jewish day school has its roots in the European setting of yesterday. The pioneer Jewish day schools in the United States were patterned after the 19th century European yeshiva, the traditional institution of intensive Jewish studies. The chief subjects were *Pentateuch* (written law) in the lower grades, *Talmud* (oral law) in the middle and upper grades, along with their traditional rabbinic commentaries. The immigrants who founded the first yeshivot in the United States at the end of the nineteenth and beginning of the twentieth centuries were motivated by the tradition of Torah learning as they had known it in Europe. For them, as for their ancestors, Jewish education occupied a unique position, as a cardinal principle of Jewish faith. The combination of Judaic and secular subjects under one roof also had antecedents in Eastern and Western Europe where several such institutions existed.

The Jewish day schools in America are generally independent, autonomous institutions, founded and supported by autonomous, self-governing lay boards. (That is why we do not refer to them as "parochial schools," since that term implies control by a central church or parish.) Their autonomy is reflected in the variety of the educational programs and in the patterns of program scheduling. The Hasidic and ultra-Orthodox yeshivot and Beth Jacob schools (representing about one third of the total Jewish day school enrollment) are single-sex institutions. In addition to the regular state-required general education program, pupils in the all-boys yeshivot are exposed to Judaic studies twenty to forty hours per week, including a full day of Jewish learning on Sundays—primarily *Pentateuch*, Codes, *Talmud* and their commentaries—all in the original Hebrew and Aramaic. The curriculum of the girls' schools comprises *Pentateuch* and commentaries, *aggadah* and *midrash* (legends relating to the Bible), Jewish history, ethics and Hebrew religious literature.

Most of the modern or centrist Orthodox Jewish day schools (comprising about one half of the total day school enrollment) are co-educational institutions. Their programs feature a balance between Judaic and secular subjects. Jewish studies (15–25 hours per week) include Hebrew language and literature, *Siddur*, *Pentateuch*, Prophets, Writings, *Talmud* and their rabbinic commentaries, Codes, ethics, Jewish history, the Land of Israel and Jewish music.

The Conservative Solomon Schechter schools (with about 10 percent of the enrollment) are all co-educational institutions with balanced Judaic and secular programs. The Hebraic curriculum (12–15 hours per week), is similar to the modern Orthodox programs, with less emphasis on *Talmud* and rabbinic commentaries and greater stress on conversational Hebrew.

The Jewish studies curriculum of the communal inter-ideological day schools (with about eight percent of the enrollment) is similar to the Jewish studies program of the Solomon Schechter schools, but with less time devoted to *Pentateuch* and *Talmud*.

The Jewish day schools under Reform auspices (two percent of the enrollment) provide a combined Judaic and general studies program with five to ten hours of Jewish studies, centering on Hebrew language, Bible, Jewish holidays, Jewish history, Jewish current events and Jewish arts.

The dramatic growth of Jewish all-day education began in the 1940s, as Orthodox Jews began establishing day schools despite the indifference, and even opposition, from the rest of the Jewish community. Their championship, sponsorship and support of the day school idea, abetted by a considerable Orthodox birthrate, is largely responsible for the flowering of Jewish all-day education. The remarkable continued growth of this movement was further aided by the support from leaders of Conservative Judaism and the founding of Conservative Solomon Schechter schools since 1957, by the recent interest of Reform Jewish leaders in Jewish all-day education, and by the financial assistance of Jewish communal Federations throughout the North American continent. The recent recognition of the value of intensive Jewish education for Jewish continuity and the enhancement of Jewish life has also intensified the interest in and support for all-day Jewish education.

To be sure, other factors have also contributed to the initial and continuing growth of the Jewish day school. These include the impact of the Holocaust, the founding of Israel, the perception of violence and drug use in public schools, the rise of fundamentalism in America, the attractiveness of the general studies programs of many day schools, and the search for cultural identity.

Questions Raised by Jewish Day School Growth

These two opposing trends—the deterioration of the Jewish supplementary school on the one hand, and the growth of all-day Jewish education on the other—give rise to several questions that beg for answers, particularly in light of claims made by supporters of day school education about its impact upon the adult Jewish lifestyle of its graduates.

What role does a Jewish day school experience play in the Jewish identity of its exponents? What other factors contribute to the development of the Jewish life style of young Jewish adults? Is the Jewish behavior of Jewish day school graduates related to their home backgrounds? To Jewish camp experience? To Israel visitation? To study in Israel? What kind of Jewish behavior do young adults who attended Jewish day schools exhibit? Do those who attended for longer periods of time demonstrate higher levels of Jewish observance and involvement? What are the marriage patterns of graduates? How do they feel about intermarriage? How frequently do they intermarry? What kind of Jewish education do or will Jewish day school graduates give their own children?

Ample research evidence shows a statistically significant relationship between Jewish all-day education and adult Jewish behavior. Jewish day schools certainly have an important bearing on friendship patterns, prevention of intermarriage, attitudes towards intermarriage of progeny, visits to Israel, Shabbat and kashrut observance and synagogue attendance, among others.

Time spent in school, by most accounts, has a significant influence on Jewish identity formation, even when a variety of factors (including family background) are controlled. The research of Rimor and Katz claims that nine or more years of schooling is critical. Others, including Goldstein and Barak Fishman, suggest a minimum of six years is important.

The longer one stays in school, the stronger the relationship between day school attendance and adult Jewish behavior and involvement, regardless of the school's Jewish religious ideology, the background of the parents, or other factors. In other words, adult Jewish behavior and involvement increases with the length of stay in Jewish schools. The level of Jewish behavior increases with the extensiveness of Jewish education. Elementary school has a basic effect; secondary school has a cumulative effect; and post high school, a multiplier effect on adult Jewish behavior.

Moreover, the combination of intensive formal Jewish education, a positive Jewish home and sound informal Jewish educational experience contributes significantly to the development of positive adult Jewish behavior. But whatever the combination of factors, extensive Jewish day school education is the most important single contributor to the formation of strong Jewish identities.

The fact that 100 percent of the graduates do not exhibit Jewish behavior, despite long years of schooling, demonstrates that even a Jewish day school education is not a foolproof guarantee of Jewish continuity. Neither schooling alone, however powerful a weapon, nor any of the other factors, taken in isolation (such as family background, camp attendance, Israel visits, religious affiliation in later adulthood, and Jewish organizational involvement) can completely counteract the influences of an open society on young people.

To be sure, some Jewish behavioral gain might not be due to education and/or home. There also seems to be some loss (however small) of Jewish behavior, among some graduates, despite the home and despite the educational grounding. It would be impossible to expect full retention from generation to generation. Some loss from the ranks in more observant sectors is natural, as well as gains in Jewish behavior from non-observant groups. Such loss and gain are normal facts of life, and do not themselves endanger the continuity of the Jewish community.

On the whole, the evidence is strong that Jewish day school education helps graduates retain Jewish attitudes and behaviors experienced during their upbringing, while reducing negative attitudes about Jewish behavior, Jewish identity and Jewish life that may have been acquired in the larger environment. And if an extensive Jewish education is bolstered by a positive family environment and other Jewish experiences, it will prevent further erosion and contribute significantly to the continuity of American Jewry.

Because the research data indicates so clearly that extensive Jewish all-day education is an indispensable tool for the formation, reinforcement and continued vitality of Jewish identity, the organized Jewish community is increasingly concerned about all levels of Jewish day school education.

The American Setting

The Jewish day school is founded on the principle that a synthesis of religious and secular culture is the necessary basis for a Jewish child's adjustment to his larger American environment. While the idea of a synthesis of disciplines was born in Western Europe, the integration of Jewish tradition and American civilization could only flourish on American soil.

The significance of the principle of synthesis lies not in its uniqueness or soundness as a theory, but in the framework of its implementation. What makes the idea of synthesis a valuable and workable theory for American Jewry is the fact that the integration of the general and religious disciplines takes place in a Torah environment.

Projected into long-range focus, the principle of synthesis not only serves as the basis for creative Jewish survival, but also plays a significant role in the cultural development of the general American community. In the words of Dr. Joseph H. Lookstein, one of the pioneers of the Jewish day school movement, this institution "is destined to become a major contribution of American Israel to American cultural democracy."

As the American Jewish community has matured, most of those who were concerned with the Jewish day school's rivalry of the public school gradually shed this feeling. In the first place, the long Jewish romance with the public school has cooled off. Secondly, since Jews constitute less than two percent of the American population, even if all Jewish children attended Jewish day schools, this would hardly make an appreciable difference in the public school population nationally. Locally, too, the absence of all the Jewish children from public schools would not be a cause for concern. Even in Greater New York, where the Jews constitute about fifteen percent of the total adult population, the attendance of the entire Jewish child population in Jewish day schools would not endanger the status of public education.

The leaders of the Jewish day school movement see it as an important force in the American educational scene. This point was clearly underscored during the early growth of the day school in the United States by one of its pioneers, Marvin Fox. In 1953, Dr. Fox optimistically suggested that the most important single area in which the day school could make a significant contribution to American education is in counteracting the philosophy and practice of "value-free education." "By reminding America constantly that there are legitimate ways for man to understand himself and his world other than through the insights of scientific naturalism, the day schools can help to avert the dangers of the kind of intellectual totalitarianism which no democratic society can afford. This is the first and most fundamental contribution of the Hebrew day school to the pattern of American education."

Fox also believed that the day school would set an example in the matter of discipline, by demonstrating how Judaism reconciles "human equality with reverence for authority," and how "this view expresses itself through acceptance by the young of parental authority and of the authority of the teacher." And in a more general way it should serve as "an important bulwark against the terrible moral confusion of our time. . . . Through the medium of the sacred writings in their broadest scope, the Jewish school tries deliberately to endow its students with moral knowledge and even more, to develop in them moral sensitivity."

Whether or not Dr. Fox's hopes have been realized, the Jewish Day School's intensive dual curriculum has certainly demonstrated, contrary to the opinions of the advocates of "relaxed programming," that pupils do not buckle under a heavy, full-day course of study. The yeshiva has shown, beyond a shadow of doubt, that children can readily master a foreign language, even at a tender, primary school age. The Hebraic program of studies has demonstrated that pupils, adequately oriented, can learn abstract material in the elementary grades that is far more theoretical and more difficult than the subject matter of their parallel general studies classes. For example, the introduction of Talmudic study on the fifth and sixth year level has clearly shown that the elementary school child is capable of abstract and creative thinking far beyond the current educational diet to which he is exposed on the elementary level and even on the secondary level. In this sense, the Jewish day school bears out the long-held contention of some educators and psychologists that, given the right conditions and taught by the proper method, children at any age can be instructed in almost any subject matter ranging from animal husbandry to metaphysics.

The Jewish day school reaffirms the old pedagogical truth that good learning takes place best in an intimate environment. The traditional Judaic concept of personalized instruction is one of the earmarks of the modern Jewish day school. The contrast between this aspect of the teaching-learning situation in the day school and the kind of pupil-teacher relations that generally pervade the large urban public schools is readily observable.

However, it must be noted that whatever influence the day school may have upon the general American scene, that is only secondary and incidental to its major purpose and function. The real vital impact of this institution is upon the Jewish community.

Support From All Quarters

Because of the value of Jewish all-day education to the Jewish community and to American society as it educates generations of good Americans, good bread winners, and good people, the sponsors of this form of education favor increased support for it from every possible source—the family, the school board, the Jewish community and the public sector (where this support does not do violence to the concept of separation of church and state).

The Jewish community has been and remains steadfast in its championship of the separation of church and state. However, like Catholic and Protestant sponsors of non-public schools, Jewish day school advocates strongly favor all forms of governmental help to their institutions—direct aid, books, materials, facilities, transportation, free and reduced school food programs—based upon the pupil benefit theory. They all agree that school aid or scholarship assistance to the non-public school must be limited to the general, secular education of the recipients of that assistance.

This has been adequately underscored by the education laws in every state that recognizes the legitimacy of such schooling and makes provisions for its supervision. The Department of Health, Education and Welfare has provided loans to private non-profit schools under the National Defense Education Act. Moreover, the federal government and many states authorize tax exemptions for non-public and non-profit educational purposes.

The American setting encourages each minority group to maintain its own integrity and identity, and to contribute from its own traditions and creative forces to the mainstream of American life. The Jewish day school is one of the ways in which the Jewish community maintains its integrity and encourages its own singular creativity while benefiting American society.

The Financing of Jewish Day Schools

Marvin Schick and Jeremy Dauber

Day Schools in American Jewish Life

The Federations are American Jewry's primary instrumentality for providing communal services. As much as the dollars which they allocate, their priorities are the barometers of what is regarded as important in organized Jewish life, a way of assessing what the community considers to be worthy of support and attention.

The place given to Jewish education on the Federation agenda—and therefore also on the agenda of American Jewish life—gave prominence to two interrelated commitments which for decades shaped the main activities of the Jewish education establishment. The first of these was the strong commitment to the ideal of professionalism, the view that, like education generally, Jewish education had to be guided by standards in teacher training and licensing, curriculum, student testing and financial accountability. Jewish education, according to this outlook, could not be conducted as a random activity by anyone who professed an interest in operating a school or teaching in a classroom.

When Federations gave financial support to the local boards of Jewish education, they were endorsing the work of professionals whose hallmark was the determined insistence that Jewish education be directed by experts who shared their vision and their notion of professionalism.

Secondly, the institutional expression of this commitment was a strong preference for after-school programs which were generally known as Talmud Torahs. They have also been referred to as religious or congregational schools and, more recently, as supplementary Jewish education. These were typically three-day-a-week programs conducted on Sunday morning and two afternoons during the week for Jewish students who attended public schools, with the usual focus being on the upper elementary school years, as students approached their Bar/Bat Mitzvah. There were variations on the theme, as in the once-a-week Sunday school programs which found favor in Reform Jewish ranks.

The preference for *Talmud Torahs* captured the imagination of the Jewish masses, as well as the educational elite, for it allowed for a measure of religious training consistent with the great and virtually unchallenged American Jewish commitment to public education. This commitment was a cornerstone of the American Jewish ideology. All educational developments, whether in the Jewish or general domain, were evaluated in terms of their consistency with the profound belief in the moral and social utility of public education.

Supplementary education was the overwhelmingly favorite mode for educating Jewish youth. Relatively few children attended yeshivas or the more modern day schools, a pattern that probably would not have been much altered had there been less hostility at the time to this more intensive mode of formal Jewish education.

It should be noted, because it is relevant to the contemporary picture, that, for the most part, Jewish schools, including *Talmud Torahs*, were not the direct recipients of Federation funding. The financial responsibility for maintaining supplementary schools rested primarily with the sponsoring organizations, most often a congregation, and the parents through their tuition payments. Federation subventions essentially went to the boards of Jewish education to help cover their operating budgets and the services that they provided to schools.

After World War II, there was a considerable increase in the number of day schools, nearly all of which were sponsored by the Orthodox. This trend has continued unabated for more than four decades, with more recent developments indicating a growing interest in day schools in non-Orthodox sectors. Although the statistics of American Jewish education are generally not reliable, the best indications are that there are now nearly 200,000 students in more than six hundred Jewish day schools, ranging from pre-school through the high school years.

These numbers suggest some of the daunting problems inherent in the financing of Jewish day schools, for many of these institutions have very small enrollments in comparison to public school enrollments.

As more students have enrolled in day schools, there has been a concomitant shift in communal attention to their needs. The Federation world's attitude toward day schools was profoundly affected by the changing mood in American Jewish life. This is an ongoing process for which an equilibrium has yet to be established and, indeed, may never be established. Still, it is possible to delineate two distinctive phases in the creation of a new, more favorable, Federation attitude toward Jewish day schools.

In the earlier stage, American Jewry moved away from its universalistic agenda toward more particularistic concerns. This process was forged by a confluence of social and psychological circumstances, including growing Jewish insularity arising from American Jewish concerns about Israel and Soviet Jewry, as well as such potent domestic issues as urban unrest, Black Jewish relations, anti-Semitism, Jewish poverty, neighborhood instability and much else.

Obviously, this new mood was also fed by the growing ethnocentricity which enveloped American ethnic groups in the wake of the Black revolution. The old idea about the melting pot was discredited and replaced by the notion that each group had the right and obligation to fend for itself.

The second and still evolving phase of shifting Federation priorities was in response to the growing alarm about Jewish population statistics. The 1990 National Jewish Population Survey (NJPS) was the seminal event, but much else that was alive in American Jewish life contributed handsomely to the view that the organized community was obligated to take urgent steps to promote Jewish identity, commitment and continuity.

At first impression, this new climate of heightened concern regarding advanced assimilation and the abandonment of Judaic commitment should have benefitted day school education. To quote from the 1994 report of the Jewish Education Service of North America (JESNA), "The current consensus across virtually all segments of the community is that the day school is the most effective 'formal' Jewish educational mode, and will continue as such in the foreseeable future." Presumably, the alarm about Jewish continuity, when linked with the new consensus about the effectiveness of day schools, should have been translated into massive Jewish philanthropic action to assist these schools.

Nevertheless, it is clear that there has not been a wholesale transformation in funding formulas in favor of day school education. Upon reflection, it is equally evident that a transformation of this magnitude could not readily come to pass, no matter the urgency or the rhetoric or the consensus.

For one thing, the new and sincere concern of the Federation world about Jewish continuity has unhappily coincided with stagnation in Federation fundraising, with most projections suggesting that the likelihood for an upturn is dim. In this regard, Federations may be viewed as another victim of advanced assimilation, as Jews with diminishing Jewish loyalties cannot be expected to contribute to Federation or most other Jewish causes. In fact, one of the startling findings of the NJPS was how few American Jews contribute to Jewish causes.

At the same time, Federations have been adversely affected, perhaps paradoxically, by the spreading tendency of Jews of both great wealth and strong Judaic commitment to channel their philanthropy through private or personal foundations. This has deprived Federations of a customary source of significant income.

Thus day schools have gained greater acceptance in American Jewish life at a time when competing communal pressures have placed enormous difficulties in the way of a substantial reallocation of philanthropic resources towards day schools.

The Study of Day School Finances

Federations continue to be the best barometer we have for measuring trends in American Jewish philanthropy. What they do regarding day schools is apt to tell as much about the larger picture of how private Jewish philanthropy is responding to these institutions.

Probably the best current source of information on Federation funding of day schools is JESNA's 1994 report, which was based on research conducted in 1992. Thus, the data collected about Federation allocations could not have been more than minimally affected by the sad story revealed not much earlier by the NJPS. JESNA's study relied entirely on what Federations themselves reported about their allocations to day schools, a perspective that is understandable in view of JESNA's linkage to the Federation system.

JESNA received information from sixty-five Federations outside the New York area, representing about forty percent of the approximately 160 Federations in the United States.[1] The responding communities represented 164 schools, about forty percent of all day schools outside of New York. In 1992, these institutions enrolled 41,500 students or about 23 percent of the students attending day school in the U.S.; again, if New York is excluded, the figure rises to probably 35–40 percent

JESNA found that for the 65 responding communities, nine percent of the "total campaign" was allocated to Jewish education, of which about half went for day schools. Day schools located in small communities fared somewhat better than those located in larger communities, which JESNA interpreted as possibly indicating that "there is a greater reliance on communal support for Jewish education in smaller communities because of the limitation of other resources and sources of support." Another and perhaps more reliable explanation for this pattern is that the smaller communities had no more than one day school to support, a conclusion that is buttressed by other JESNA data.

JESNA found that the average per capita or per student cost in day schools ranged from $6,400 in the very small schools which enrolled 75 or fewer students, to about $5,000 in most other day schools. For all 164 schools, Federation allocations amounted to $530 per student or about ten percent of the average per capita cost. As a percentage of the budgets for the 164 schools, Federation support amounted, on the average, to 12.3 percent of the total.

Our survey, sponsored by the Avi Chai Foundation, covers the 1995–96 school year, and is an effort to examine Federation funding and day school finances from the perspective of the schools. Questionnaires were mailed to about 400 day schools in the United States outside of the New York Federation service area. Ultimately, we received 160 completed questionnaires, of which 154 could be used. This figure is only slightly below the 164 schools covered by JESNA's study. The 154 day schools are served by approximately 97 Federations, which is to say that this study involves a very large proportion of the Federations which have day schools in their catchment area. The 1995–96 enrollment in the 154 day schools came to 42,000, about the same as JESNA's figure.

The Underfunding of Day Schools

In the aggregate, day schools are underfunded, their budgets have been rising and their income is derived primarily from tuition and other parental charges. Also, their financial stability depends on philanthropic support and the success of their fundraising.

When day school budgets are examined in raw terms without regard to the dual—and therefore more expensive—nature of their educational program or without regard to school size, and then compared with the budgets of public and private elementary and secondary schools, the inescapable conclusion is that many, perhaps most Jewish day schools are forced to live a parsimonious existence.

JESNA found that excluding the very small institutions, the average per capita operating costs for schools in its survey came to about $5,000. Our study, conducted four years later, has produced somewhat, but not greatly, higher figures. The per capita or student cost in our 154 schools ranged from a bit more than $6,000 in the Community schools, to about $5,000 in the small number of Reform day schools, and between $5,500–$6,000 in the Solomon Schechter and Torah Umesorah schools. The low figure for Reform day schools is explained by the high percentage in these schools of pre-school children, for whom the per capita cost is significantly lower. The highest per student expenditures occur in the larger schools, which tend to have the most varied programs and offer the highest salaries.

As a generalization, the underfunding of day schools encompasses nearly all of these institutions, irrespective of their affiliation or size. When day school budgets are examined without regard to affiliation or size, the annual per capita cost in 1995–96 amounted to between $5,400 and $5,600, which suggests (based on JESNA's figures) that in the 1990s, per capita costs have risen at the rate of two to three percent a year.

Most day schools are located in states which spend heavily on public education, and in more affluent communities where per student expenditures are almost certainly higher than what they are in the neighboring Jewish day schools. Yet the claim of underfunding is not predicated exclusively on comparative budgetary statistics. When the dual educational nature of the Jewish schools is factored in, their budgetary differential with private and public schools becomes far more glaring. A dual curriculum always means two sets of faculty, and in many institutions it also brings another layer of administrative personnel. Faculty and staff salaries and benefits comprise by far the lion's share of the additional costs. However, the non-personnel costs also add up, including textbooks, study and library material and even the additional maintenance and utility expenses resulting from the typical day school operating longer hours.

The consequences of underfunding are neither abstract nor minor. Underfunding affects nearly every aspect of day school operations, probably most notably the salaries paid to faculty. With relatively few exceptions, Judaic studies faculty are underpaid, at times severely, a situation that is universally acknowledged, even as it is lamented. Matters are not better, and they may be worse, at the general studies staff level.

Underfunding also affects, probably more severely, the availability of auxiliary course offerings for gifted and special students, as well as to make the academic program generally richer and more varied. Remedial education in many day schools consists of a limited resource room, while supplementary courses and enhancement programs of the kind that are routine in top-flight public and private schools are rare. Budgetary constraints allow the typical day school to provide only a basic curriculum and not much more.

To an extent, fiscal limitations are overcome by the commitment of teachers, administrators, parents and students, indeed, by the total day school environment, which makes the learning experience challenging and effective. It is a tribute to day school education that students appear to be strongly motivated and high achievers.

It is an exercise in self-delusion to believe that the underfunding of day schools does not exact a cost, both in the substance of the educational program and in the perception that many parents have of the relative benefits of the day school versus the competing public or private schools. Unhappily, this is evident in the enrollment curve. As grade level rises, enrollment declines.

Tuition

The lion's share of the day school budget must be met by tuition. Those responsible for day school education have come to believe that however important a religious Jewish education is from the communal perspective, it remains a service being provided to consumers who happen to be parents, and who should be charged for this service as they would for any other.

Increasingly, tuition charges are pegged to the actual cost of a day school education. Day schools are even taking punitive measures (denying admission, withholding report cards and diplomas, and barring students from taking tests) to make parents pay what the schools regard as a fair share. These deprecations are justified by the financial hardship facing so many schools, and yet they remain deprecations.

For the non-Orthodox, who constitute by far the largest potential pool of day school students, there is a distinctly greater possibility that tuition charges may well be a deterrent, if only because historically the non-Orthodox have shied away from Jewish day schools. Logic suggests that tuition is a disincentive for these Jews. Tuition is probably a stronger force in restricting day school attendance as the degree of religiosity becomes weaker. Reports from several communities—Denver, Seattle and Montreal, for example—indicate that tuition is an important but not exclusive consideration. A study commissioned by the Samis Foundation of Seattle shows that when tuition is lowered, enrollment goes up.

Day school officials say that prospective parents who opt against day schools usually give tuition and the unavailability of adequate scholarship assistance as the reason. Yet relative to other private schools, Jewish day schools are liberal in granting financial aid. But parents say that they have been humiliated when they applied for assistance and sometimes offer their experience as the reason, indeed the justification, for deciding against, or at times withdrawing their children from, day school.

Finally this: as economic forces drive up the cost of day school education, there is almost certainly a correlation between this form of education and socio-economic status, much in the same way that there is a correlation between other private education and socio-economic status. This does not mean that people who aren't affluent are excluded from the world of Jewish day schools. As we know, Judaic commitment is the primary determining factor of parental choice. But it may be that as day school education becomes a real option for Jews of marginal religiosity, as with much else in organized Jewish life, the people who are less affluent are more likely to turn away from Judaic involvement.

As a way of holding down tuition increases without holding down income from parents, day schools have become creative, even bold, in imposing charges that straddle and probably obscure the boundary between tuition and fundraising. In addition to various supplementary registration fees, many institutions impose, for example, a mandatory dinner contribution (typically calculated as the cost of two dinner reservations), building fund charges, and a requirement to purchase supermarket coupons.

When tuition and fee income are examined from the perspective of school enrollment, a clear pattern emerges. The percentage of the budget that is covered by parental charges increases as enrollment increases. In the smaller schools, only half of the budget is met by tuition and fees, while in the larger schools of more than 300 students, the benchmark figure of 75 percent is clearly attained. However, these schools comprise fewer than 30 percent of the day schools.

Fundraising

There is a considerable gap between day school income from tuition and fees and what it costs to provide the dual educational program that is essential to their mission. In Orthodox schools, this gap amounts, on the average, to more than forty percent of the budget. It must be bridged somehow if schools are to continue to operate.

Day schools have limited options as they seek to bridge this budgetary gap. Given the powerful strictures regarding separation of church and state, governmental funding is currently unavailable except in New York and select other locations, and there, too, only to a limited extent. This may change if the advocates of school vouchers have their way and if the arrangement can pass constitutional muster. As yet, vouchers are not available to pay day school bills. Should they ever be extended to parochial schools, a new set of dynamics or tug of war between parents and schools over tuition will likely be set into motion.

If public funds are unavailable, what remains to help pay the bills is philanthropic support and, more broadly, fundraising. This isn't a new experience. As was suggested earlier, Jewish educational institutions and especially yeshivas have long enjoyed priority status as a recipient of charitable funds. Not too long ago, these were the main source of income for Jewish religious schools. What has changed is that tuition and fees now account for most of the budget, with fundraising and philanthropy being the junior, albeit desperately needed, partner.

With whatever degree of sophistication or organization they can muster, all but a few day schools try to induce people to contribute to their cause. There are holiday mailings, raffles, occasional appeals, special events, telephone solicitations, visits to prospective large givers and, most essentially, dinners as part of the fundraising arsenal of day school officials, lay and professional, who know that their school's financial health may well depend on their efforts.

Of the many fundraising techniques, the annual dinner appears to be the most ubiquitous, maybe because dinners have become part of the ritual of organized American Jewish life. These events often do well enough to provide much of the added financial backing that is needed to eliminate the budgetary gap.

Whatever the outcome of dinners—and for day schools far more are successful than not, if only because of the mandatory charge levied on parents—they demonstrate the growing practice of making parents responsible for day school finances. In one fashion or another, the parent body accounts for almost all of day school income. Through the mandatory dinner charges, additional voluntary contributions and what they solicit from others, the dinners have emerged as parent-centered events. Understandably, much of the dinner income results from the giving and efforts of the more affluent parents who are already paying their fair share. Just the same, when parental fundraising is taken into account, day school balance sheets consist, in large measure, of parental giving and getting to a larger extent than is indicated by a reckoning of tuition and fee income.

The statistics of day school fundraising appear to be impressive. For all school categories, whether by affiliation or enrollment, more than half of the income shortfall is bridged by contributions and, in some, it is virtually eliminated.

Orthodox schools are likely to be more liberal about tuition—what they charge and how insistent they are about collecting what they charge—because they intuitively understand that a considerable portion of their income comes from contributors, which is the way they believe it should be. Other day schools do not have this history of relying on charity and they are not overly receptive to the notion of raising money for basic operating expenses. They calculate their budgets by focusing almost entirely on tuition fees, raising them when necessary to cover increased school costs.

For most schools, large-scale donations are received only occasionally. Overall, fundraising is hard work undertaken by volunteers and top staff, often including the school principal. Most contributions are relatively small, burdening the office staff which must keep records and send out acknowledgements. In day schools and yeshivas where fundraising is an ongoing central concern, the attention and resources devoted to it can detract from other important business, including the academic program.

The pattern of fundraising can result in financial instability. When so much depends on charitable gifts, a downturn in contributions has serious consequences for a school's program, in the same way that reduced enrollment can wreak havoc with a school. It is not uncommon for day schools to cut back in mid-year because they haven't raised sufficient funds to close the budgetary gap.

Instability in fundraising could be offset by endowments, as it is in many major cultural and educational institutions. The catch, of course, is that few yeshivas or day schools have endowments of a sufficient magnitude for the income to make much of a difference. We believe that within the day school world, meaningful endowments are currently the exception and not the rule.

Many day schools may live too close to a hand-to-mouth existence to have the luxury of an endowment fund. Furthermore, some day school offices may not yet have conceived of the possibility of the approach. If they would focus a bit on the idea, many would find that implementation is not all that formidable. Any serious effort to improve the financial lot of day schools by confronting the problems that result from underfunding, must give high priority to the promotion of the idea of endowment funds within the day school world.

Federation Support of Day Schools

For all day school categories, no less that five-fifths of the budget is covered by what parents pay and income from fundraising. For many schools, the figure is nearly 90 percent or higher. Under these circumstances, how important can Federations be in the economic profile and planning of day school education?

In fact, the Federation role may be decisive.

For openers, ten percent (or certainly more) of a school's budget is not an inconsequential figure. This small proportion can help to stabilize or upset the institutional budget. If a day school has a budget of one million dollars, the people who are responsible for the institution's management rarely have to fret over more than ten percent or $100,000. If the needed funds come from a single source—for example, the Federation—the school's income matches its outlays and this had been accomplished without an inordinate expenditure of time and other scarce resources.

Beyond this, Federation support goes to the heart of the issue of educational underfunding. Federation allocations can do more than plug budgetary holes; they can provide for programmatic expansion, the upgrading of facilities and other enhancements which make these institutions more suitable to the middle class or upper-middle class comparison shoppers who are their prospective parents.

Finally, Federations are barometers for trends in Jewish philanthropy. Accordingly, their role is powerfully symbolic. When they downplay day schools, as they did for so long, they are sending a message to the organized Jewish community and particularly to its philanthropic sector that, at best, day school education is one more item on a long list of activities and institutions with hat in hand seeking alms from Federations and donors. However, when Federation increases its funding or contributes generously, the message being sent out is that meaningful religious Jewish education has achieved status and legitimacy in American Jewish life.

The primary form of Federation allocations is the basic grant, essentially an annual subvention received by the school from Federation. Whether it is calculated according to enrollment, or more likely, simply a reflection of what Federation decides to give the school as it distributes available funds to agencies within its service area, the basic grant is direct assistance whose purpose is to help the recipient institutions meet its financial obligations. It is not targeted toward specific activities and generally does not come with any programmatic strings attached.

All but eleven of the 132 day schools which received direct Federation support were given basic grants by their local Federations. Furthermore, for about 40 percent of the recipient institutions, the basic grant came to more than $100,000. On its face, this appears to be a high, even impressive, figure, although it does not take into account school size or other factors which may help determine the impact of the grant on a school's financial situation.

Fewer than a handful of day schools received any capital or building fund support. The degree of support picks up for scholarship assistance, with twenty day schools reporting Federation grants for this purpose. Only in the grants for Russian and other special students was the number of beneficiary institutions substantial. Fifty-five day schools said that they have received this form of assistance; for more than sixty percent of these schools, the grant level was above $10,000 per school.

Federation involvement in day school education through auxiliary activities such as Israel experiences, summer camping and family education is minimal. There is a slightly higher level of involvement regarding curriculum and teacher training, but these are services that have long been offered by local boards of Jewish education as an aspect of the allocations which they receive from Federation.

Community and Orthodox schools do appreciably better in garnering Federation support than their Conservative and Reform counterparts, which isn't surprising since they are far more likely to be in single-day school communities and also because they tend to be more aggressive in seeking communal philanthropic assistance. Community schools are the most favored by Federation, apparently because they are transdenominational and purport to serve the entire religious spectrum. The low figures for Reform and Orthodox institutions can be accounted for by their relative newness and perhaps also by their innate tendency to rely almost exclusively on tuition and fees to cover their operating budgets.

Since the jolting revelations of the NJPS and its aftermath, as well as the corollary new enthusiasm for day school education in quarters where it was once denigrated, we might expect this new mood to be translated into increased Federation allocations. The data, however, is mixed, providing support for differing, even contradictory interpretations of trends in Federation allocations.

Thus it is possible to read the fixed dollar statistics as showing a distinctive trend in the direction of increased funding, for nearly twice as many day schools report increased allocations over those which report decreases. However, by a wide margin of 78 to 50, the schools report that there was no increase in fixed dollars.

When Federation support is calculated as a percentage of the day school budget, relatively few schools (only seventeen) report an increase, while a clear majority of schools report that Federation support has decreased.

Many factors have to be considered in understanding the possible obstacles to Federation funding of day schools. These include stagnation in Federation fundraising, competing priorities in education, continuity and outreach, and the inability of Federations to turn away from prior commitments. In addition, the growth in the number of day schools and in enrollment has restricted what Federation can do for recipient institutions, particularly on a per pupil basis.

Conclusion

The essential purpose of this report was to examine the structure of day school finances. One theme which emerges from these pages is that day schools are, with relatively few exceptions, seriously underfunded. This truth cannot be news to people who work in day schools or who are responsible for day school financing. The challenge that faces all who care about day school education is to confront this issue, for unless it is confronted, most American Jews may never consider this form of education, and even when they do, will not elect it. Day schools will remain institutions that are praised in the abstract but ignored when parents actually choose where to educate their children.

Endnote

1. Because New York is "sui generis," JESNA did not include the New York Federation of Jewish Philanthropies in its study. With perhaps 250 day schools and as much as one-third of the entire day school enrollment in its catchment area—both figures are more than ten times the number for any other Federation—New York's Federation is confronted by a situation that is radically different from what prevails anywhere else, and inclusion of its data would have distorted the findings.

Dollars and Day Schools:
The Baltimore Experience

Jay Bernstein and Larry Cohen

Introduction

The major challenge facing American Jewry today is continuity. The open, democratic society we live in has taken its toll on American Jews, as reflected in the soaring rates of assimilation, intermarriage and non-affiliation. One institution, however, has succeeded in stemming the tide, and in meeting the continuity challenge. That institution is the Jewish day school.

Among all segments of the Jewish community, there is a consensus that the day school is the most effective formal Jewish educational mode. Research published in 1994 by the David J. Azrieli Graduate School of Yeshiva University confirms that all-day Jewish education yields far more pronounced Jewish behavior and attitudes; reduces negative perceptions about Jewish identity and Jewish life; and motivates students to be positively inclined towards Jewish values and observances. In short, the day school has demonstrated convincingly that it is "a most effective instrument for transmitting the Jewish heritage to Jewish youth," and that it consequently is "a significant method of helping to ensure American Jewry's fruitful continuity." (Alvin Schiff, *Issachar American Style* (1988))

Advocates for Leadership in Educational Funding ("ALEF") was founded in 1996 by parents of day school students in Baltimore in order to promote initiatives for making Baltimore's Jewish day schools financially stable and affordable. Baltimore is the home of nine day schools which serve nearly 4,500 Orthodox, Conservative and Reform Jews. Despite their vital role and record of success, many of these day schools—and the families whose children attend these schools—are in crisis. Increased enrollments have resulted in increases in educational expenses, capital expenses, and in financial-aid needs, all of which outpace the income received from ever-increasing tuition charges. The resulting financial burden upon both schools and parents threatens the very survival of the day school system, and with it, the future of the Baltimore Jewish community. In order to counter these trends, ALEF has concentrated its efforts upon two initiatives: (1) increasing the amount of money allocated to day schools by the organized Jewish community; and (2) obtaining state funding of the non-sectarian needs of students who attend non-public schools.

The Underfunded Jewish Day School

The dire condition of Jewish day school education in America is described in the September, 1997 study by Marvin Schick and Jeremy Dauber issued by The Avi Chai Foundation, entitled, *The Financing of Jewish Day Schools.*[1] The data contained in the study is based upon the 1995–96 school year, and was obtained from questionnaires completed by 154 day schools outside of the New York City area.

According to the Avi Chai study, when the budgets of Jewish day schools are compared to the budgets of public and private elementary and secondary schools, "the inescapable conclusion is that many, perhaps most Jewish day schools are forced to live a parsimonious existence." The $5400–5600 cost per day school student is comparable to per student expenditures in public elementary and secondary schools, which are not burdened with the expensive dual curriculum educational programs offered by Jewish day schools. Even more glaring is the discrepancy between the per student expenditures of Jewish day schools and non-sectarian private school, which often compete for the same students. Data compiled by the National Association of Independent Schools shows per student costs which are nearly double those of Jewish day schools.

Schick and Dauber cite three adverse effects of day school underfunding. First, both Judaic studies faculty and general studies staff are underpaid. Second, the underfunding of Jewish day schools "affects the availability of auxiliary course offerings for gifted and special students, as well as to make the academic program generally richer and more varied." Due to budgetary constraints, typical day schools "provide only a basic curriculum and not much more." Third, and perhaps most important, underfunding adversely affects the perceptions of many parents regarding the relative benefits of the day school versus the competing public or private school. "Unhappily," states the Avi Chai study, "this is evident in the enrollment curve. Day school enrollment is pyramidal, with a strong pre-school base. At that level, parents generally view the day school as a form of private education, with the Jewish component as a bonus. As grade level rises, enrollment declines."

Income from tuition is insufficient to close the gap between Jewish day schools and other forms of private education. The Avi Chai study discloses that

Jewish day schools "receive far less from their parent body than what it takes to provide a day school education." For a large majority of Jewish day schools, income from parents covers two-thirds or less of their already underfunded budgets, and in Orthodox schools, the gap is even higher. These conclusions are echoed on a local level by Baltimore's Council on Jewish Day School Education. The Council reports that despite significant tuition increases in past years, "tuition fees alone cannot keep pace with increased per pupil costs incurred and underwritten by day schools in the course of their annual operations."

The tuition charged by Jewish day schools threatens to limit this type of schooling only to those who are able to afford it. According to the Avi Chai study, for 1995–1996, the average tuition was $5,131 at Orthodox schools, $5,465 at Reform schools, and $6,083 at Conservative schools. These rates not only impose a severe financial hardship on parents who send their children to day schools, but effectively exclude many parents who would like to send their children to day schools, but simply cannot afford to do so.

Communal Support for Day School Education in Baltimore

The charitable needs of Jewish communities throughout the United States are centralized in the "Federation," which collects funds for distribution to local Jewish institutions and to Jews in Israel. Avi Chai stresses that Federation funding is crucial to revitalizing the day school. The study concludes that Federation support "goes to the heart of the issue of educational underfunding, which we believe to be perhaps the most critical element in day school finances and the major factor in reducing the attractiveness of these institutions to marginally religious persons." As a practical matter, writes Avi Chai, Federation funding can "provide for programmatic expansion, the upgrading of facilities and other enhancements which make these institutions more suitable to the middle class or upper middle class comparison shoppers who are their prospective parents." Furthermore, when Federations contribute generously to day school education, a powerful message is sent that "meaningful religious Jewish education has achieved status and legitimacy in American Jewish life."

Last summer, the Associated Jewish Community Federation of Baltimore took out a full page advertisement in the local Jewish newspaper proclaiming that its "historic commitment to Jewish education" was its "highest priority." However, the numbers tell a different story. The Associated's current budget for fiscal year 1998 allocates $914,965 to day schools—the same amount as the prior year, despite a $24 million fundraising effort that topped last year's total, and less than the amounts allocated for fiscal years 1996 ($943,263) and 1995 ($1,053,263). The current budget allocation for day school education continues a long-term, downward trend; over the past five years, the Associated's allocations for day schools have decreased by 7.6 percent, even as pupil enrollment has increased by 25.3 percent, and even as total fund raising levels have increased.

The sorry state of communal support for day school education in Baltimore is confirmed by data compiled by the Jewish Educational Service of North America (JESNA) in its May, 1994 report entitled, "Federation Allocations to Jewish Day Schools: Models, Principles and Funding Levels." Based upon JESNA's data, just 5.6 percent of the funds allocated by Baltimore's Federation for local needs are distributed to day schools, compared to the national average of 12 percent. On a per-child basis, the Associated's allocation of less than $200 per day school student is far below the $580 averaged by Federations nationwide. Finally, current allocation levels do not come close to covering 12 percent of individual school budgets, which is the national mean of allocations, and which is the figure that, per JESNA, "should serve as the norm, or starting point, for any community seeking direction in these matters."

Since its formation two years ago, ALEF has embarked upon a major effort to raise the community's consciousness of the extent of day school underfunding and to press the Associated to increase its allocations for day school education. A major step towards these ends was achieved this past Chanukah, when ALEF brought together rabbis and lay leaders from Baltimore's Orthodox, Conservative and Reform communities to sign a full page advertisement in the Baltimore Jewish Times calling upon the Associated to renew and intensify its support of Jewish education.

Models for Funding Day School Education

Allocation of communal funds directly to Jewish day schools is but one way to alleviate the current crisis. The UJA-Federation of Jewish Philanthropies of New York has funded the creation of half a dozen new day schools, and provides $3.3 million a year to other day school related activities. Most recently, in October 1997, the New York Federation opted to join ten philanthropists to form the "Partnership for Excellence in Jewish Education." The Partnership plans to create a $36 million endowment designed to increase meaningfully the number of non-Orthodox Jewish youth in day schools, and to increase the quality of all day schools. Michael Steinhardt, founder of the Partnership, has declared that "the Jewish community will be transformed if access to day school education becomes the birthright of every Jew in the United States and Canada."

Similarly, the creation of day school endowments by local Federations is the ultimate goal of the National Jewish Day School Scholarship Committee. The more than 200 delegates representing communities from across the country who attended the Committee's inaugural meeting in September 1997, agreed to the need to "create special giving programs to draw on the vast untapped reservoirs of Jewish wealth that are currently ripe for productive charitable deployment to establish permanent endowments for day schools." As a first step towards actualizing this goal, the Committee has called upon Federations nationwide to pass a formal resolution committing their leadership, as one of its highest priorities, to develop long range solutions to the crisis in the funding of Jewish day school education.

In some parts of the country, private groups have responded where Federations have not. Funding provided by the Samis Foundation in Seattle has allowed the Northwest Yeshiva High School to reduce tuition from $7,500 to $3,000 per student. In California, discontent over the level of Federation funding for day schools has resulted in the formation of the United Jewish Education Fund of Los Angeles, which plans to raise money to help subsidize tuition costs.

Finally, at least a portion of the financial burden associated with day school education can be alleviated by means of public assistance. State aid for the non-sectarian needs of non-public school students is constitutional, and is provided for by 37 states. Maryland is not among these states which currently provide non-sectarian assistance, nor is the organized Jewish community in Baltimore among the groups which have recognized the benefits of seeking such assistance. In January 1997, the Baltimore Jewish Council, which is the community relations and political arm of the Associated, voted 20 to 6 against requesting state aid for non-public school students. This has placed the BJC at odds with ALEF, which has joined the effort mounted by Catholic school parents in Maryland to obtain state aid.

Non-sectarian State Aid for Students of Non-public Schools

The constitutionality of state aid to students attending non-public schools is well settled. Over fifty years ago, in *Everson v. Board of Education* (1947), the Supreme Court ruled that the Constitution does not prohibit state funds from being used to pay the bus fares of parochial school students "as part of a general program under which it pays the fares of pupils attending public and other schools." The Court noted that such legislation "does no more than provide a general program to help parents get their children, regardless of their religion, safely and expeditiously to and from accredited schools." The Everson decision was followed by the Court in *Board of Education v. Allen* (1968), which upheld a New York statute requiring local school authorities to lend textbooks free of charge to all students, including those attending parochial schools.

Based upon these precedents, some 37 states currently provide assistance to non-public school students. Nineteen states provide funding for textbooks, more than thirty states cover the cost of remedial and diagnostic services, and 21 states provide bus transportation. In the Northeast, examples of such assistance include New Jersey, and Pennsylvania, each of which allocates over $50 million to furnish students in non-public schools with textbooks, transportation, and nursing services. New York requires school districts to provide non-public school students with the same textbooks and nursing provided to public school students, and all non-public school students are transported up to a maximum of fifteen miles from their homes to school at no cost.

In Maryland, the constitutionality of state aid to non-public schools has been upheld by the Attorney General on several occasions. Citing *Everson* and *Allen*, Maryland's Attorney General has opined that "there is no doubt" that proposed legislation which would provide funds for school lunches to children attending both public and non-public schools is constitutionally permissible. (59 Op. Att. Gen 135 (1969).) The same conclusion has also been reached regarding proposed legislation directing that transportation, textbooks, instructional materials and equipment be furnished to children attending non-public schools. (59 Op. Att. Gen. 209 (1974).) In the latter opinion, the Attorney General distinguished between legislation furnishing state aid to non-public school students, which is constitutional, and statutes which provide direct aid to non-public schools, which "are held unconstitutional on the grounds that they do not provide adequate safeguards against use of the direct aid for religious purposes." (*Id* at 211.)

Notwithstanding its unquestioned legality, and the ample precedent of other jurisdictions which provide such aid, to date the State of Maryland has failed to allocate any funds for non-public school students. Last year, ALEF joined the campaign launched by the Maryland Federation of Catholic School Families requesting $14 million from the state for transportation, textbooks and technology (*i.e.*, computers) for students attending non-public schools. As part of that campaign, ALEF submitted petitions to the Governor signed by over 2,500 Jewish Marylanders calling for nonsectarian state aid to students attending non-public schools, and rallied with the Maryland Federation of Catholic School Families in Annapolis last February. During the rally, large checks made payable to the state were displayed to represent the money saved by the state by virtue of Catholic and Jewish school students not attending public schools. At an average cost per public school student of over $6,500, Jewish schools save the state at least $44.5 million, and Catholic schools save the state over $392 million each year.

Despite the petitions, rallies and lobbying, Governor Parris Glendening declined to allocate budget funds for the nonsectarian needs of non-public school students in 1997. The ostensible reason for this decision was lack of funds; by letter to ALEF dated January 22, 1997, the Governor wrote that "The constraints on the state's budget will not permit us to undertake the new major aid programs you have requested." In 1998, even though the state enjoys a $283 million surplus, the Governor's proposed budget still contains no funding for students of non-public schools. For this reason, ALEF and the Maryland Federation of Catholic School Families again rallied in Annapolis this past February in continuation of the campaign for state funding of Maryland's non-public school students. Significantly, many of the legislators lobbied by ALEF have stated publicly, this year for the first time, that they would support the Governor's budgeting of funds to provide transportation and textbooks to students in non-public schools.

Conclusion

The crisis faced today by Baltimore's day schools is not a new one. In *The Making of an American Jewish Community: The History of Baltimore Jewry from 1773 to 1920*, Dr. Isaac Fein writes that the financial situation of Baltimore's day schools was "never good." At the turn of the century, "the common plight of all schools was the lack of funds. There were always those who fruitlessly complained that the day school was the stepchild of the community's religious life." As the end of another century approaches, it is time for this complaint to be at long last put to rest. Whether by means of Federation funding, private endowments, or state aid, the means are available to end the day schools' stepchild status. Until this is done, and until all students who seek it have access to an affordable and properly funded Jewish education, ALEF will continue to raise the consciousness of Baltimoreans concerning the plight of the Jewish day school.

Endnote

1. A shorter version of this report is contained in this section of the present volume *The Financing of Jewish Day Schools* by Marvin Schick and Jeremy Dauber, p. 145 ff.

Jewish Day School Funding

George Hanus

We are known as the People of the Book, but most of our children do not know how to read the Book, and many barely recall its title. In secular terms, we are the most cultured, best educated and wealthiest Jewish community in history, but we are not educating our children Judaically. Jewish culture is languishing and Jewish illiteracy is rampant.

There is a crisis in our community. Rampant assimilation and intermarriage are obvious to all and, tragically, accepted by far too many. These phenomena, coupled with our indifference, portend the systemic decimation of the American Jewish community. Our young people, immersed in secular culture and values, are not connecting with our heritage. Jewish leadership, especially the American philanthropic community, must prioritize this need and dedicate resources, energy and facilities commensurate with the immense loss that threatens us. We must educate our children. Day school education must be available to all families who seek it, irrespective of their financial resources.

The National Jewish Day School Scholarship Committee (NJDSSC) is a national organization that brings together hundreds of lay leaders from across the country who are focused and energized to give the American Jewish community a fighting chance at survival by ensuring that every child has an opportunity to attend a day school. We have presented a resolution for adoption by every Federation in the United States as an opportunity to crystallize their position on funding Jewish day school education and raise their "continuity" rhetoric to the level of effective action. The NJDSSC will be launching a national initiative with the creation of a network of local endowment funds.

Before a problem can be solved, there must be a common language and understanding of the extent and nature of the problem. The proposed resolution clearly delineates the problem and commits the Federations to implementing the solution, embracing wholeheartedly the precept contained in the *Shema* of *v'shinantam l'vanecha*, "and you shall teach your children diligently."

The resolution affirms the proposition that Jewish day school education for our children is essential to ensure Jewish continuity. It affirms each community's obligation to make a quality Jewish day school education available to all, without regard to financial resources. The availability of Jewish day schools must be treated with at least the same urgency as other communal needs such as housing the homeless, feeding the hungry, and caring for the sick and elderly. By adopting this resolution, Federations in a number of cities, including Chicago, Columbus, Phoenix and Ft. Worth, have already committed their lay and professional leaderships to the fulfillment of these objectives and the development of a long range solution to this crisis in 1998–1999. The resolution has been endorsed by leaders of the Orthodox, Conservative and Reform movements, including Rabbi Norman Lamm (President, Yeshiva University), Rabbi Ismar Schorsch (Chancellor, Jewish Theological Seminary) and Rabbi Eric Yoffie (President, Union of American Hebrew Congregations).

History will judge the American Jewish community and its leadership on their response to these challenges. It is critical that we create a clear record of where each local Federation and its leaders stand on this resolution. We are entitled to accountability and clarity in understanding the position of our philanthropic leadership. We must know what the community spends its money on and what it chooses not to fund. Both Federation staff and lay leaders must be held accountable for their positions and funding priorities.

The day school funding crisis must be the urgent concern of every Jew, regardless of denomination, regardless of day school patronage, in every community of each region throughout this country. We must address the problem collectively with the same alacrity, conviction and resourcefulness we have mustered in dealing successfully with other Jewish crises (such as the plight of Russian Jewry), and with other basic needs of our fellow Jews (such as the Jewish poor, elderly and sick). Our local children are no less deserving, and the danger is no less imminent.

We must maintain a single-minded focus on day schools and resist the tendency to subsume all school issues under the generic heading of Jewish education/enrichment. For all their merits, supplementary schools, Israel experiences, summer camps and adult education represent distinct approaches that deserve separate attention, but they cannot be counted on to reverse the tragic trend toward the extinction of American Jewry. The effort for day schools must not be distracted or diluted by a global approach to education/enrichment.

The American Jewish community must demand of its leadership an absolute focus on the solution to this problem. We must demand that all Federations enact and implement the proposed resolution. Adoption of this resolution by Federations nationwide will sound a clarion call of national unity behind a clearly articulated goal; a prelude to resolute action and positive change.

When Federations consider this matter, we urge that they beware of specious arguments which unfortunately continue to surface occasionally from questionable quarters and suspect motives. We ask that Federations reject categorically the claim that day schools should not be substantial Federation recipients because day school parents are not significant Federation givers. Any donor-recipient linkage is anathema to a true philanthropic enterprise. We do not stop to examine the giving or other credentials of the recipients of Federation supported social services or programs which care for the aged, the hungry and the sick. Many day school parents voluntarily devote between $6,000 and $10,000 per child annually to the cause of Jewish continuity, in the form of non-tax deductible day school tuition, before the Federation pledge forms have even been mailed. To turn against them the inevitable economics of their personal financial commitment to Jewish survival is simply unconscionable.

We further ask Federations to repudiate the notion that day schools are not worthy of significant support because only a minority of our children, mostly Orthodox, attend them. Over the past 30 years the number of Jewish children in day schools has tripled, while the number in supplementary schools has fallen by more than half, and unprecedented numbers of Reform and Conservative day schools are opening every year. Studies show that day school enrollments would increase significantly if the burden of tuition were reduced. High tuition represents a significant entry barrier that must be removed so that day schools of every denomination can welcome previously excluded children from all backgrounds into their embrace. Furthermore, the transdenominational support of this Resolution has been astounding as evidenced by the letters of recommendation from leaders of the three national movements.

We must establish a clear record of the current position of our philanthropies. This declaration of principle must be voted up or down. We demand a roll call vote. Every voting member of every board and every institution from every community must clearly set forth for historic review his or her position on day school education. Both the Jew of today and the historians of posterity must be able to assess how the assimilation rate of American Jewry got out of control, notwithstanding our vast collective financial and human resources. They must be able to identify the positive or negative contributions of the current leadership to the eradication of this scourge. We will allow no wiggle room in the response. This is a yes or no vote. Each institution either passes the resolution or does not pass the resolution. There has been talk enough; essay answers are inadmissible. Individuals and institutions that assume leadership roles will be called to account for their votes. There will be no place to hide, no anonymity. Every individual leader in Jewish philanthropy must stand up and be counted.

The practical implementation of this initiative will require a major financial commitment, the magnitude of which could reach billions of dollars in potential endowment fund requirements.

There are those in our community who believe that the source of funding for Jewish education should be through vouchers. The National Jewish Day School Scholarship Committee believes that discussion of vouchers at this time is premature. There are significant constitutional issues that legal authorities dispute and the issue has created an emotional divide in our community. We do not believe that the endorsement of vouchers at this time adds to a meaningful resolution of the controversy. We cannot wait for that issue to be resolved before we act on our own behalf.

We believe that the long term solution is the creation of Jewish education trust funds. The National Day School Scholarship Committee is proposing the establishment of regional endowment funds along the following model.

Within the next decade, the largest intergenerational transfer of wealth in the history of the world will occur. A significant portion of this wealth must be dedicated to establishing Jewish Education Trust Funds to subsidize day school tuitions and to provide scholarships for Jewish children of needy families, in perpetuity. The principal of the funds shall never be distributed; only the income of the funds shall be used. The NJDSSC will attempt to create such a fund in every city in the U.S.

These funds will provide a singular opportunity for donors to create a living legacy for future generations. As the survival of the Jewish community faces the increasing threats of assimilation and intermarriage, it is imperative that we create strong, financially sound and affordable Jewish day schools. The NJDSSC will hire planned giving experts to go to every city that has a day school to assist the leadership in setting up these endowment funds. We are hopeful that strategic alliances with the local Federations will be formed in order to maximize energies and efficiencies.

Jewish leadership must take bold steps now to solve these enormous problems. Empirical studies and evaluation of data already abound. There is no need, or time, for further investigation of the problem or the alternatives. Any factional divisiveness or internecine warfare is foolish and destructive. *Achdut* (unity) in leadership, commitment and focus will produce the necessary solutions. This enterprise is going to take enormous cooperation and resources. Some may say that the Jewish community cannot afford the billions of dollars necessary to ensure success. The fact is that we cannot afford to do otherwise. Current leadership must either commit itself fully to assuming this responsibility now, or else step aside in favor of those with the conviction and vision to act now for our future.

THE SCHOOL VOUCHER DISPUTE

Elliott Abrams

The argument over school vouchers raises three highly controversial points for American Jews. The first is relations between Orthodox and non-Orthodox Jews; the second is which of two rival faiths, Judaism or secularism, will win more support among American Jews; and the third is whether secularism will prove so strong as to trump even traditional Jewish liberalism.

Orthodox and Non-orthodox Jews

The heart of the Orthodox community is its private school system. Where once a full yeshiva education was reserved for the small percentage of the population preparing for the rabbinate, today a K–12 day school system includes the vast majority of Orthodox youth, and many from non-Orthodox homes, male and female. In fact, full-time Jewish education in America today remains largely Orthodox education: 500 of the 625 Jewish day schools in the United States are Orthodox. Of all the children attending Jewish day schools, 68 percent attend Orthodox schools, while only 15 percent attend Conservative-run schools, 14.5 percent attend community sponsored multi-denominational schools, and just 2.5 percent attend day schools sponsored by the Reform movement.

The commitment to a separate school system has marked off the Orthodox from the rest of the Jewish community. In fact, as the mostly Orthodox day school enrollment has risen, attendance by mostly non-Orthodox children at afternoon or Sunday Hebrew School classes has dropped, a "reflect(ion of) the polarization that is occurring among American Jews between a religiously devoted minority and an increasingly secularized majority."[1]

This polarization has had a large impact, in part because most American Jewish organizations have staked out positions far more supportive—whatever their rhetoric—of the large portion of American Jews offering their children little or no Jewish education. Given the importance that religious schooling holds for the Orthodox, it is vital to gain access to the taxes they pay to support the public schools they do not use. But the major American Jewish organizations have been unremittingly hostile to this desire, as their briefs and their alliances in the important Supreme Court cases have demonstrated. The bitter division between Orthodox and non-Orthodox Jewish groups was clear in 1993 in California, where a ballot proposition would have provided every student with a tuition voucher that could be used at secular or religious schools. Backing the initiative (known as "Proposition 174") were the Union of Orthodox Jewish Congregations, Agudath Israel of California, the Rabbinical Council of California, and Chabad-Lubavitch. Opposing it was virtually every non-Orthodox Jewish organization, including the Jewish Federation Council of Greater Los Angeles, B'nai B'rith, Hadassah, the (Reform) Union of American Hebrew Congregations, the American Jewish Congress, and the American Jewish Committee.

American Jewry has been remarkably unsupportive of religious education. One need only compare the attitude of the Catholic Church toward its own day schools to see the difference. The Jewish newspaper Forward reported on January 13, 1995 that "private Jewish day schools are considerably more expensive than their Catholic counterparts." Moreover, "few sources of financial aid are being made available to Jewish families who long to give their children Jewish educations but can't afford the steep prices." Scholarship funds exist but are "hard to obtain, and the process of application is daunting and humiliating." The director of one Jewish day school told the Forward that enrollment could be doubled if tuitions could be brought down. The more expensive Jewish day schools, such as New York's Ramaz school, charge a high school tuition of $12,500 per year, an amount simply unheard of among Catholic day schools (where high school tuition is typically about $3,000). Such scholarships as are available often focus on new immigrants, and rich families can pay the tuitions, leaving the middle class high and dry. Thus a family earning $50,000 or $75,000 per year, having three children, and trying to save for their college education cannot possibly afford ten, twenty, or thirty thousand dollars for secondary school education.

What we see is the portion of the American Jewish population that is most successful in retaining the loyalty of its youth—the Orthodox—fighting for funds to support the schools that are central to that effort, and being opposed by the rest of the Jewish population. It is possible, of course, to argue that day schools are terrific but should be supported exclusively by private Jewish funds. Some non-Orthodox Jews do make this argument, and support has been growing for several efforts, such as that of the National Jewish Day School Campaign. The goal is to raise endowment funds for day schools and to ask each city's Federation to pledge itself to the goal of making day schools affordable through the provision of Federation support funds. It is striking indeed that the leaders of the Conservative and Reform movements have endorsed these efforts, and have declared day schools "kosher" and highly desirable. But at least until the late 1990s, the pattern drawn earlier has prevailed. Day schools remain largely creatures of the Orthodox movement and are critical to its success, and receive little support from non-Orthodox Jews. Is it unfair to suggest that they have received little support because they are critical to Orthodox success? And that non-Orthodox Jews must change their attitude from rivalry, or even prejudice, to support of more observant fellow Jews.

Secularism vs. Jewish Continuity

But Rabbi Schorsch of the Jewish Theological Seminary and Rabbi Yoffie of the Union of American Hebrew Congregations are right: day schools are critical. The fight about day schools and school finances is central, not marginal, to the future of American Jewry, for religious education is invaluable in transmitting Judaism from one generation to the next. If day schools have been an Orthodox matter, they must now become part of non-Orthodox life as well.

"Jewish education," the National Jewish Population Study revealed, "is one of the most effective tools for producing Jewishly identified adults, (and) more extensive forms of Jewish education are closely associated with greater Jewish identification." Not surprisingly, Jewish education seems to reduce intermarriage as well. Sylvia Fishman and Alice Goldstein of Brandeis report that the impact of extensive Jewish education "is demonstrated in almost every area of public and private Jewish life . . . (E)xtensive Jewish education is related to a greater ritual observance, greater likelihood of belonging to and attending synagogues, greater levels of volunteerism for Jewish causes, and greater chances of marrying a Jew and being opposed to intermarriage among one's children.[2]

If the Jewish community is serious about its continuity and survival, support for day schools is an essential step. Not because most American Jewish children will attend them, even if tuitions are low. Today, despite reasonably low tuitions, only about one-fourth of all Catholic elementary school age children attend Catholic schools, and the figure is less than 20 percent for high school age children. The vast majority of Jewish day schools in the United States are Orthodox yeshivas, and it is nearly impossible to conceive of circumstances in which majorities of non-Orthodox children would attend day school. But with better funding and more community support, more would do so than do today. This would strengthen the American Jewish community, because day school graduates will be well-educated Jews and, as the data show quite conclusively, are far more likely to be observant Jews, marry Jews, and raise their children as Jews.

Secularism vs. Liberalism

Until now, the American Jewish community has itself funded day schools poorly, and at the same time strongly opposed any form of tax relief or tuition vouchers that would help the Jewish parents trying to pay for them. The vehement opposition of the Jewish establishment and Jewish liberals to school vouchers that would, in the main, go for religiously sponsored schools is especially notable because it trumped arguments that might otherwise have appealed to their liberalism. After all, the Catholic schools that would receive the bulk of such vouchers are the only alternative for many ghetto parents seeking to keep their children out of disastrous public schools. Often the school population in inner-city Catholic schools is substantially non-Catholic, including many non-white Protestant students seeking a better education. In fact, according to Kosmin and Lachman, 23 percent of all students in Catholic schools are non-white, and 12 percent are non-Catholic. A remarkable two-thirds of black students in Catholic schools are non-Catholic.

The most striking discussion of the issue of public support for religious and private education came in a May 1994 speech at Princeton University by Diane Ravitch, a former Assistant Secretary of Education and, until then, a staunch critic of tuition tax credits, vouchers, and other plans to provide financial relief for parents with students in non-public schools. First Ravitch explained that it was no answer to say "improve the public schools," because decades have passed without that incantation having had the slightest impact. Instead, the public schools seem to get worse. That is why so many families want to escape them. "It is not just," she said, "to compel poor children to attend bad schools. It is not just to prohibit poor families from sending their children to the school of their choice, even if that school has a religious affiliation. It is not just to deny free schooling to parents with strong religious convictions, any more than it would be just to prohibit the use of federal scholarships in non-public universities (like Notre Dame, Marymount, Yeshiva, or even Princeton)."

Ravitch then wondered what we mean by "public school," anyway: "Thus, the paradox: a school in an exclusive suburb that educates affluent students at a cost of $15,000 per student per year is 'public,' while an inner city parochial school that educates impoverished minority students at a cost of $2,000 per year is not 'public.'"

Wealthy families can choose private school, or move to the suburbs, but the inner-city poor have no choice—unless something like a voucher system gives it to them. That solution would allow observant Jewish parents some relief as they seek a Jewish day school education, and could be of real assistance to the poorest parents as they, too, try to give their children the kind of start in life they most value.

Such an argument would seem likely to appeal to American Jews not only as Jews but as political liberals; but Orthodox parents find that it is rejected out of hand. In 1995 Rabbi Alan Silverstein, President of the (Conservative) Rabbinical Assembly, argued against vouchers on the grounds that "only in destitute, inner-city neighborhoods will public vouchers for the proposed $500 per child enable poor children to opt for low-cost private education. Certainly in the suburbs, several hundred dollars is not the breaking point between attending or avoiding prestigious prep schools." Here a Jewish religious leader argues against vouchers despite their admitted usefulness for the poorest children, on the grounds that they do little good for the suburban rich!

No accommodation is permitted; in the view of most Jewish groups, the wall of separation must be an iron curtain. Nor can this position be defended by a simple reference to the Constitution, as if current interpretations of that document by the Supreme Court were cast in iron and not subject to challenge or change. In fact, most American Jews are very likely unaware of the bizarre state of the law regarding support for parochial schools. As Robert Bork succinctly described it several years ago, "where religion is concerned . . . a state may lend parochial school children geography textbooks that contain maps of the United States but may not lend them maps of the United States for use in a geography class; a state may lend parochial school children textbooks on American colonial history but not a film about George Washington; a state may pay for diagnostic services conducted in a parochial school but therapeutic services must be provided in a different building."[3]

Jewish opposition to aid for religious schools cannot, then, be defended as "mere" constitutionalism. There is a great argument over what the Constitution says on this matter. The current state of the law is extremely convoluted, and Jewish attitudes reflect powerful policy preferences rather than conclusions ineluctably drawn from the First Amendment. Most strikingly, they reflect a deeper commitment to absolutism in separation of church and state than to liberalism, if the latter can be defined to require helping the most disadvantaged citizens. Many Jews and Jewish organizations have been blind to the positive impact vouchers might have on poor Black and Hispanic children, and have hidden their eyes behind the most extreme separationist arguments.

Perhaps, to switch metaphors, the log-jam is now breaking up. Clearly the value of day schools for Jewish continuity is now understood by many non-Orthodox leaders, and the last few years have seen rapid growth in non-Orthodox day schools. Perhaps this alone will cause some change in the Jewish community's attitude toward vouchers. Active espousal of vouchers (and of other school reform measures, such as charter schools) by Black leaders and white liberal politicians would no doubt set many liberal Jews to rethinking as well, for it would show that their views on this issue contradict their professed concern for the disadvantaged.

Will this happen? Optimism seems better justified than pessimism today, for the dire consequences of public school monopolies in central cities, and the inestimable value of Jewish day schools, are undeniable even to liberal and secular Jews. Tune in in ten years and Jewish attitudes and spending patterns will look very different.

Endnotes

1. Barry A. Kosmin and Seymour P. Lachman, *One Nation Under God* (New York, 1993), p. 271.

2. Sylvia Barack Fishman and Alice Goldstein, "When They Are Grown They Will Not Depart: Jewish Education and the Jewish Behavior of American Adults," Cohen Center for Modern Jewish Studies, Research Report no. 8 (March, 1993), p. 12.

3. Robert H. Bork, "What To Do About the First Amendment," *Commentary*, vol. 99, no. 2 (February 1995), p. 23.

The Jewish Community and School Choice

Jonathan S. Tobin

Why do most mainstream American Jewish organizations and their constituents oppose school choice programs?

"Because Rev. Pat Robertson wants to overthrow our democratic way of life and install a Protestant theocracy in which the Christian Coalition will rule and American Jews will be a despised minority without equal rights under the law. Any deviation from a strict separation of church and state will enable Robertson and the unwashed hordes of Middle America who watch his "700 Club" television program to unleash their anti-Semitic vision and end America as we know it. Enact school choice and kiss your rights goodbye."

"Because if school choice becomes legal, then extremists like African-American racist Louis Farrakhan and his Nation of Islam, as well as white supremacist groups like the Militias, will use government funding to train a new generation of black and white children to hate democracy and the Jews. The breakdown of the public school monopoly would mean that democratic values will no longer be part of the educational experience of American children. Thus Jews, who benefitted greatly from the acculturation process provided by the public school system earlier in the century during the time of mass Jewish immigration, will be marginalized in American society."

Are American Jews frightened by school choice? Given these fantastic and utterly unrealistic scenarios, of course they are. And as long as a rigid ideological commitment to separationism is the foundation of the American "civic religion," opposition to choice will remain widespread.

The use of these scare tactics and red herrings remains the backbone of the campaign against school choice in the Jewish community.

In analyzing the debate as it has unfolded between, on one side, the vocal minority of American Jews who have come to doubt the separationist faith and, on the other side, its high priests in the American Jewish Congress and the Anti-Defamation League, the falsity of these claims is almost beside the point. The twin specters of Pat Robertson and Louis Farrakhan are enough to convince many Jews that their rights really are hanging by a thread, and that it is only strict separationism which prevents American democracy from dissolving into a cesspool of sectarian anarchy.

Equally appealing to the imagination of most American Jews is the veneration of the public school system, which is apparently threatened by vouchers. The devotion of Jews to public schools as "temples of liberty," Rabbi Isaac Mayer Wise said a century ago, should also not be underestimated.

Only a generation ago, Jewish religious schools were confined to a minority of the most fervently Orthodox communities. The only large-scale parochial school system was Catholic. It was seen by most Jews as exclusionary and a danger to democracy and therefore to the Jews. Only the public schools guaranteed Jews a place in American society.

Though these circumstances have changed, the knee-jerk reaction of Jewish liberals to the possibility of opening up educational choices to parents has not. They still thrive on the annual "December dilemma" controversies in which Jews see themselves as threatened by the imposition of Christmas trees and carols on innocent Jewish eyes and ears. Indeed, as some wags in the Jewish community see it, without this annual Jewish communal conniption fit, some elements of American Jewry would have no way to express a distinct identity!

However, separationism—taken in moderation and with common sense—still is an important concept in law and public policy. American Jews continue to look to the U.S. Constitution for the protection of minority rights against the possibility of majority misrule. Issues such as sectarian school prayer are rightly seen as threatening to the rights as well as the sensibilities of Jewish students and parents.

But more and more American Jews are beginning to question the theology of strict separationism, the veneration of the public schools, and the validity of these scare stories about the threat which extremists would pose to their liberties if choice prevails. That is because rigid separationism—the fundamentalism of the liberal intellectuals—is coming into conflict with two of the Jewish community's vital interests.

The first of these is American Jewry's increasing stake in the survival and growth of the day school movement.

In contrast to the not-so-distant past, the greatest problems facing American Jewry are not those of domestic anti-Semitism or threats to Jewish populations abroad. In the face of spiraling rates of assimilation and intermarriage, anyone who is serious about the continued survival of American Jewry knows that Jewish day schools—whose numbers are growing every year—are essential to the Jewish future. The sort of comprehensive Jewish education that these schools provide is the best—and perhaps the only—real antidote to the ignorance and apathy that afflicts contemporary American Jewry.

Unfortunately, the cost of this education is prohibitive for most middle class Jews. It may be argued, with much justice, that the primary responsibility for alleviating this burden rests on the Jewish community itself and specifically on Jewish Federations—the Jewish umbrella fundraising organizations. But given the failure of most Jewish Federations to address this need by making day schools a top priority, many Jews have turned to vouchers and school choice plans as a possible alternative.

School choice has the potential to make Jewish day schools an affordable alternative to public schools. Yet even the fact that these schools might be a crucial factor in addressing American Jewry's most pressing problem has not been enough to change the opinions of a Jewish leadership still wedded to the problems and solutions of the past.

A second pressing Jewish interest which dictates support for school choice has less to do with the parochial concerns of the Jewish community than it does with a question of American social justice, a matter of vital importance (and therefore of conflict) to Jewish liberals who oppose choice.

The plight of children stuck in inner city schools in a state of collapse is not something that Jews who care about the future of the cities as well as the rights of the underprivileged can afford to ignore. Public education, once the hallmark of an upwardly mobile society, has deteriorated to the point where it has become a death-trap for America's poorest citizens.

In places like Hartford, Connecticut, where city schools are almost totally segregated by race and are academically suspect (one of the largest public high schools in Hartford was actually de-certified by state academic authorities in 1997), it is clear that the public system is failing the overwhelmingly minority student population. Some ideologues would prefer to divert the discussion of this issue into the intellectual dead-end of racism or to calls for increasing the already sky-high budgets of urban public schools. Ironically, Hartford's public schools have achieved the distinction of having the lowest academic ratings and the highest funding levels of any school district in the state.

The real alternative is to offer inner city parents a choice and therefore a chance for their children to succeed. School choice offers parents and students the opportunity to decide where they will get the best schooling. By forcing schools to compete for students, choice would open up the education system to the genius of the marketplace, which has worked wonders elsewhere in American society. This is a principle which has made American universities the envy of the world.

Experimental choice programs, such as the pioneering program offered in Milwaukee, the proposals offered for the District of Columbia, and the privately subsidized choice plan in New York City, offer choice only to the disadvantaged. While such programs would not alleviate the financial burden of private schooling for most Jews, it does offer hope to minority youngsters. African-American leaders such as former U.S. Representative Floyd Flake of New York and State Rep. Polly Williams of Wisconsin have spearheaded a growing movement in the minority community in favor of choice.

A Jewish community committed to the concept of social justice must ask itself at some point whether it is prepared to offer minorities more than platitudes about separationism and big government solutions that have already failed. Jews have a moral obligation not to stand in the way of the struggle of inner city students for a decent education.

Given the need, for reasons of our own continuity, to create concentrations of Jewish population, Jews also need cities and therefore ought to be committed to their survival. School choice options for parents can help keep urban neighborhoods alive and therefore should also command Jewish support.

In the words of Barry Shrage, the influential president of the Combined Jewish Philanthropies of Boston, it is time for a "reassessment" of the Jewish community's opposition to school choice.[1] Although a great supporter of day schools, he believes the factor that will motivate Jews to support choice is our passion for social justice. The plight of America's most disadvantaged students shows that "there is a prima facie need to increase the experiment" of school choice.

Contrary to the doomsayers, choice will not destroy the public schools but will allow competition to make them better. Nor will it compromise our constitutional rights. School choice will not empower extremists but will empower parents of every race and religion to help save their children. A Jewish community which believes that these children, all children, are made in the image of God, cannot afford to stand in the way of choice for narrow ideological reasons.

School choice is not a panacea for the ills of America's urban areas any more than it is a magical solution for the problems of Jewish continuity. But it is a healthy step in the right direction which deserves a full trial. For the most parochial as well as the most universal of reasons, American Jews ought to support school choice.

Endnote

1. Barry Shrage's remarks are contained in his contribution to the roundtable discussion included among the papers of this section.

Rethinking Vouchers

Avram Lyon

A small, vocal segment of the Jewish community is in favor of school vouchers. The overwhelming majority of Jews, however, are not. Given the problems facing many urban school systems and given the Jewish community's longstanding commitment to social justice, they encourage the Jewish community to reconsider its tradition of opposition to school vouchers, and instead to support a plan that would allow parents to use public tax dollars to help pay for tuition at religious and other private schools. Vouchers, they suggest, would give low-income parents more control over their children's education and would allow at least a few children to escape inadequate inner-city public schools.

Theirs is like the cry of the bewildered and befuddled liberal, wringing his hands, not knowing what to do, or of part of the religious segment of the American Jewish community, desperately seeking to justify public funding for yeshivas or Jewish day schools. They conclude that society should divest itself of its responsibility to provide universal public school education and turn the job over to parents. Give them vouchers and "fartig."

Universal public school education, however, is an integral part of the American promise and of the social contract which exists between and among the people of this nation. We cannot, and dare not, abrogate this responsibility. Furthermore, we know what to do. We just need the courage to do it.

Vouchers don't work.

According to a study done by Professor John Witte of the University of Wisconsin, after four years students in the Milwaukee voucher program are doing no better than their public school peers—and in some cases they are worse off. Furthermore, the NAACP and other major African-American community agencies see vouchers as inherently unfair to poor inner-city children and vehemently oppose them.

The real questions we should be asking are these: What is right with our best schools? How do we apply the lessons learned from successful schools to failing inner-city schools?

Successful schools, wherever they are, share a few common attributes: (1) a safe environment and stable school/student relationship; (2) a disciplined environment for learning; (3) a first-rate curriculum; and (4) high academic standards.

All this is, and should be, obvious. If you were successful in school, you probably attended an institution that had all or at least most of these attributes. You didn't change schools multiple times during the year. Disruptive behavior was not tolerated. Your school had a curriculum that made sense and taught you how to think. Finally, your school had high academic standards and you were encouraged to reach your full potential.

This first point, a safe and stable school/student relationship, is crucial. Inner-city schools are often characterized by student populations "on the move." It is not uncommon for inner-city schools to see a thirty to seventy percent change in population during the academic year. (One inner-city Milwaukee school reported a one hundred twenty percent change in student population during one year!) By contrast, the student turnover rate in most suburban schools is about three percent per year.

The most talented and inspiring teachers in the world cannot teach effectively if they face a student population change of more than twenty percent over the school year. The ability to transmit knowledge, and the students' ability to learn, will be severely and negatively affected. School classrooms are mini-social equations, and if you constantly change the numbers in the equation, then the outcome originally anticipated is unlikely to be achieved.

Here is one solution to problems caused by mobility.

Inner-city children who take part in magnet school programs in Milwaukee seem to fare far better than their peers. Magnet schools—specialty schools such as language immersion schools, schools for the arts or sciences—draw their students from all over the city. Students are bused to these schools no matter where they live. The waiting list for such schools far exceeds the number of desks available. Inner-city school children seem to thrive in these environments. Why?

First and foremost, the magnet school is a safe and stable environment. No matter where the students live or how many times their families may move, the school bus picks them up at their new home and takes them to the same school every day. In fact, the school may be the only stable environment the students experience.

Vouchers, however, are not the same as magnet schools. Vouchers are a popularity contest between schools. The voucher concept also assumes that a poor, single, inner-city mother, now part of a workfare program and trying desperately to get off public assistance, has the time to analyze the advantages and disadvantages of myriads of schools.

Voucher proponents also assume that there are empty desks in religious and other private schools just waiting to be filled. This is hardly the case, and private institutions readily admit that they would have to "ramp up" in order to handle a large influx of students from the public school system. That would take time, talent, facilities and funds that are not immediately available.

When it comes to vouchers and public schools, America is a schizophrenic society. Most voucher proponents take for granted that children will be bused to school. Most public schools, on the other hand, are thought of as "neighborhood" schools for which busing is not necessary. We should give public schools the same advantage we would give voucher schools, and provide our children with continuity in education and a safe and stable environment where learning can take place.

Finally, despite arguments of "protections" made by pro-voucher supporters, voucher plans would make public funds available for anyone wanting to start a school—including Louis Farrakhan, the Ku Klux Klan, militia groups and the Posse Comitatus—so long as those schools meet minimal state educational standards. Those standards usually include basic skills such as reading, writing and math. They say nothing about the teaching of anti-Semitism, cultural bias or race hatred.

Public schools have traditionally been the institution of American society not only for education, but for socialization and the teaching of respect and tolerance among children of diverse social, ethnic and religious backgrounds. The unintended consequences—and perhaps for some, the intended consequences—of vouchers, could be just the opposite—the raising of ethnic barriers, suspicions, and religious hatred and fear. Voucher experiments in other countries (England and Chile, for example) have found this to be the case.

The solution to the failures of our inner-city schools lies in the attributes of successful schools. All of our schools should afford children a safe, stable environment, an environment where appropriate behavior is the standard and not the exception, and with a first-rate curriculum and high academic standards. An inner-city student should start and finish the school year at the same school, even if it means busing that child to the school.

Simplistic solutions to complex questions solve nothing. Voucher plans are simplistic solutions that don't address any of the core problems afflicting inner city public schools. It is time we faced our responsibility as a society. We know what must be done to save the future of our inner-city children and the future of our society as well. What we need is the courage to do it.

A Statement on Voucher Policy

Jewish Council for Public Affairs (JCPA)

In February 1997, the Jewish Council for Public Affairs (JCPA) embarked on a year-long reexamination of its policy regarding government-subsidized vouchers for non-public education. The study included two major components: an exploration of the many facets of the voucher debate by a national ad hoc committee; and individual review of the issue by local Jewish communities across the United States. The national committee and those communities who participated in the study process overwhelmingly concluded that:

- the JCPA should reaffirm its existing policy in opposition to publicly financed vouchers for non-public school education, because such voucher programs would undermine public education and also would violate the Establishment Clause of the First Amendment;
- the JCPA should reiterate its commitment to supporting sound, innovative educational programs that will improve public school education without compromising essential constitutional freedoms; and
- the JCPA should strongly support non-governmental efforts to provide additional financial resources for Jewish day schools and other forms of Jewish education, emphasizing that the responsibility for funding Jewish education lies first and foremost with the Jewish community.

Introduction

The ongoing debate over vouchers has particular resonance for American Jewry, as it implicates three distinct values of importance to the community: (1) support for the nation's public school system, which educated millions of Jewish immigrants and their children in this century, and where most Jewish students still receive their education today; (2) preservation of church/state separation, which has helped to foster a tolerant, welcoming society blessed with freedom of religious expression; and (3) the need to provide greater financial support for Jewish education, and particularly Jewish day schools, in the hopes of stemming the assimilation, apathy, and unfamiliarity with religious tradition that is increasingly prevalent among American Jews.

The first two principles have traditionally led a majority of American Jews to oppose the implementation of voucher programs that would provide tuition assistance for private religious school students. However, escalating concern about assimilation has led some American Jews to rethink long-held views with respect to aid to private sectarian schools, on the theory that the availability of vouchers to underwrite Jewish day school tuition would result in more Jewish children receiving a comprehensive Jewish education, thereby enhancing Jewish continuity. American Jews must now confront the challenge of balancing these diverse interests to benefit their own community and all of American society.

Public Education

The American Jewish community has traditionally placed a high value on public education. Public education serves a vital role in American society, teaching common civic values and fostering tolerance, respect and appreciation for the nation's collective diversity. In addition, public education is open to all children, regardless of their race, religion, disability, ability to pay, or other family or personal circumstance. Contrary to much of the rhetoric surrounding the voucher debate, a substantial proportion of the nation's public school system continues to provide American children with a sound education. Studies reveal that the most troubled schools are located in impoverished areas, which have been neglected or even abandoned by public officials for decades. However, even in the most blighted areas of the country, dedicated and creative educators have experienced success in implementing innovative educational programs that significantly enhance student achievement.

Notwithstanding those successes, there can be no question that poor, minority children have been disproportionately disadvantaged by the nation's neglect of its public education system. Many, if not most, Black and Latino students living in inner-city neighborhoods attend inferior public schools that lack adequate facilities, security, instruction, and books and other equipment. The organized Jewish community shares the desire of inner-city leaders, many of whom are long-time coalition partners, to respond in an immediate and bold fashion to the educational failures that disproportionately impact urban children. However, the JCPA believes that vouchers are not the panacea for dramatically improving the education of poor children or for overcoming the daunting challenges faced by urban schools. Rather, the JCPA is concerned that voucher programs are likely to:

- drain precious financial resources from public school systems, and eventually lead to even less financial and civic investment in public education;

- result in the best students, and/or those with the most actively involved parents, being "skimmed" from public schools, leaving behind those children who are not accepted into private schools or whose parents are not sufficiently involved in their children's education to take advantage of voucher programs, thereby further depressing the quality of these public schools and the life chances of their students; and,
- not provide sufficient funds to cover the entire cost of private school tuition, thereby benefiting only those parents who can make up the difference.

The JCPA strongly supports the development and continuation of quality innovative programs designed to improve public education. Many education experts believe that measures such as providing high-quality teacher training, raising academic standards, lowering class size, encouraging increased parental involvement, and permitting choice within the public school system can have a significant impact on student achievement in lower-performing school districts. These efforts are notable not only for their variety, but also because they represent a strong commitment to improving our public schools, rather than a capitulation to the perceived sense of irreversible failure that often permeates discussions about public education. At this critical juncture, the JCPA believes that it is imperative for the organized Jewish community to reaffirm its commitment to the nation's public schools, where most of its children have been and continue to be educated.

First Amendment
The JCPA and the majority of American Jews remain firmly committed to the belief that the wall of separation between church and state is an essential bulwark for religious freedom in the United States. Over the last two hundred years, the First Amendment has enabled religious life in the United States to flourish and pluralism to thrive. It has protected this nation from the bitter religious strife that to this day devastates so many areas around the world. It has gained American Jews a level of security and freedom that is unique in the two thousand year history of the diaspora.

The JCPA reiterates its long-standing belief that publicly funded vouchers used for sectarian school tuition costs seriously undermine this fundamental principle, as expressed both in the First Amendment to the U.S. Constitution and parallel provisions in state constitutions. It is the JCPA's view that whether vouchers are paid directly to sectarian schools or are disbursed to parents, the underlying effect is the same: American taxpayers are compelled to support financially, and therefore promote, religious beliefs they may not share, thereby infringing upon their religious freedom. Moreover, the government regulation that invariably accompanies the receipt of public education dollars, in the form of operational policies and procedures, curriculum guidelines, and the like, could itself lead to government interference with religious instruction and practice, further limiting religious freedom and raising questions about improper church/state entanglement.

Voucher proponents assert that such financial support is constitutionally permissible if it is provided in a neutral fashion, and is equally available to all religious denominations as well as those attending non-sectarian private schools. The JCPA emphasizes once again its view that the purpose of the Establishment Clause is not to ensure that the government adopts a neutral or impartial position with respect to religion, but that it neither promote or endorse religion nor entangle itself in religious affairs at all. Therefore, no matter how neutrally designed a particular voucher program may be, if it includes private sectarian schools, the JCPA believes that it violates the Establishment Clause, because it utilizes public funds to promote religious and religiously-based education.[1] The mission statements of private sectarian schools bear witness to the fact that for many, if not most, of them, religious education and inculcation is a primary, if not the primary institutional goal, one which is reflected in every aspect of school activity. The JCPA believes that the use of public funds to cover tuition costs at such schools is therefore irreconcilable with basic First Amendment principles that dictate the relationship between church and state in America.

Jewish Continuity

A study conducted by the Susan and David Wilstein Institute of Jewish Policy Studies and the American Jewish Committee, *Re-examining Intermarriages* by Bruce Phillips confirmed that the best strategy for stemming assimilation among American Jews is to encourage Jewish educational experiences of longer duration during the adolescent years. Such experiences include after-school educational programs, camps, youth groups, and Israel programs. The most intensive form of Jewish education is the Jewish day school experience.

Recently the organized Jewish community has begun a long overdue effort to correct chronic underfunding of Jewish day schools. Many supporters of Jewish education believe that vouchers would be another valuable tool in strengthening Jewish day schools. However, the JCPA study has raised serious questions about the potential value of vouchers to the growing Jewish day school movement:

1. Would Jewish schools that accept government vouchers be subject to greater government regulation and interference in matters ranging from space allocation to curriculum, thereby infringing upon the schools' religious and academic autonomy?

2. How many Jewish parents would use vouchers to send their children to Jewish schools rather than non-sectarian private preparatory schools?

Finally and most importantly, as a matter of principle, the JCPA believes that the responsibility for solving the crisis in Jewish education lies first and foremost within the Jewish community, and not with federal, state or local governments. The Jewish community must ensure that all of its children, regardless of family income or denominational affiliation, have the opportunity to receive a quality Jewish education, whether it be at day schools, summer camps, after-school programs, or Israel experiences. The JCPA applauds initiatives by Jewish philanthropists, educators and religious leaders to increase awareness about the need to dramatically increase the Jewish community's support for its day schools and other educational programs and to commit financial resources to achieve this goal. The failure to assist American Jewish youth in developing strong, positive Jewish identities is a communal one, and the solutions to this crisis of spirit must come from within, by devoting the same energy and sense of purpose to this issue that American Jews have brought to so many other worthy endeavors.

Conclusions

For the reasons stated above, the JCPA therefore resolves:
- to reaffirm its opposition to publicly-funded voucher programs that aid non-public schools;
- to proceed with an in-depth examination of the public education crisis in America, under the auspices of JCPA's standing Committee on Public Education;
- to recommit itself to playing a leadership role in the quest to improve American public education, by seeking sound, innovative methods of improving public schools, and actively advocating for improved budgets and other reforms at federal, state and local levels;
- to dedicate itself to addressing the need to strengthen Jewish education, primarily but by no means exclusively by ensuring adequate funding for Jewish day schools, after-school synagogue programs, summer camps, and Israel experiences; and
- to encourage Jewish community relations agencies throughout the United States to devote their energy and resources to grass-roots programs that will both improve public schools and also foster Jewish continuity.

Endnote

1. To the extent that vouchers are aimed to subsidize the secular portion of religious school education, the required governmental efforts to monitor and enforce a purely secular component would likewise result in an unconstitutional entaglement.

Remarks From a Roundtable Discussion

Melvin Shralow

The first question that has to be asked is—what problem are we trying to solve? Do we want to solve the problem of the failure of public schools in the inner cities? That is one kind of issue. Or is the problem the attempt to lighten the burden on parents who pay taxes to support public schools and then pay tuition for private schools? That needs a different approach. We've got to decide which problem we are trying to solve. I don't think that we can solve all of them simultaneously.

And we can't continue to ignore the problem of race. We all remember the famous trial that ended last year in California. A prominent criminal defense lawyer in Philadelphia, when asked by an interviewer what he thought would determine the O. J. verdict said, "Three factors: race, race, and race." We don't talk about race, yet we have to. Marc Stern pointed out today that the public schools have always tried to provide a foundation of common values in our country. Now, with the advent of multi-culturalism, some groups are encouraging separatism, which is the antithesis of the concept of the melting pot. We need to determine what we want our schools to accomplish. Isn't it their purpose to help create a basic civic and intellectual framework that Americans can agree on, even while each of us continues to have parts of our lives where we are different? Until we decide that question, we can't deal with the other issues that proceed from it.

From the perspective of the Jewish community, I think we have always looked at the First Amendment and the separation idea as a protection for our community against competition within the political arena for government support. As a small minority in this country, we have always viewed ourselves as needing protection from the imposition of religious ideas and atmosphere by the majority, predominantly Christian culture. Professor Sarna reminded us today that the earliest schools in this country were originally Protestant. In Philadelphia, I understand there were actual riots over the Catholic objection to the Protestant ethic and atmosphere in the schools. I'm told that the Catholic school system began in Philadelphia as a reaction to Protestant teachings.

The Jewish community didn't react for a long time. Then the school prayer cases provided a new impetus, and we looked to the First Amendment and the separation idea for protection in that area. But now we are beginning to hear that this very protection may be having results that are severely prejudicial to other parts of the community—the Afro-American community, the Latino community, those parts of the community that are dependent on the public school system, but are not threatened by the forces which were threatening to us. If, as I believe, we are no longer in the same danger, may we now retreat from these positions in deference to social groups who are having more severe problems than we? Or do we worry that the worm could turn? In our Jewish history, we have experienced centuries of comfort in countries from which we were eventually expelled.

There are many facets to this problem and we all have to be flexible in dealing with it. Over the years, the Jewish community has dialogued very successfully with the African-American community. We have also had very close relationships and good discussions with the Catholic and Protestant communities. And I think we demonstrated at the February 1997 meeting of the Jewish Council on Public Affairs (formerly NJCRAC) that we can also have a civil discourse on a subject like this among the various branches of Judaism. It is my hope that we can maintain and enhance the civility with which we approach these issues so that we can all find our way to compromise and ultimately do what is best for the children of America.

Barry Shrage

I spend most of my existence as Director of the Combined Jewish Philanthropies of Boston, and in that role I spend a great deal of time thinking about the challenges of Jewish continuity. Jewish education and day schools are always a very central part of that consideration. Our discussion today is not just about vouchers. It is about the future of the Jewish community.

We are not among the pessimists, we're among the optimists. I see a renaissance developing in the Jewish community, characterized by an increased interest in learning Torah and also a genuine concern for a Jewish social justice agenda. The Jewish Council on Public Affairs meeting, referred to by Mel Schralow, made a genuine and serious effort to struggle with texts. We've had a great increase in day school enrollment in Boston, particularly among non-Orthodox students. I see Conservative and Reform congregations taking their perspective on religious life much more seriously. Based upon what I view as a revolution in adult Jewish learning, I see increased numbers of Jews turning to day schools because, just as they will not permit themselves to be illiterate Jews, they certainly will not want their children to be illiterate Jews. And as we all know, Jewish afternoon schools are a very difficult place to learn Jewish values.

Although the public schools have often not been neutral about religious values, we have to agree that they have nevertheless been exceptionally good to the American-Jewish community. I believe most American Jews appreciate this. We have always been very grateful for the wall of separation between church and state. America has been good to the Jewish people and lots of American Jews believe that wall of separation is what has kept us safe here. When I talk to people, I sense that this commitment remains quite strong. Our discussion today must be held in that context.

Let me share with you that I'm a product of a day school education on the elementary school level and then, along with many of my compatriots from the yeshiva, I went to the Bronx High School of Science. There, in the ninth grade, I was put into a new environment where it seemed that half of the students were yeshiva kids and the other half were from Catholic parochial schools. We all got to know each other quite well and for the first time in my life I found out what a Catholic was. It was an interesting experience and, in retrospect, a very good one. All of us shared quite an experience that first day at the Bronx High School of Science, because our science teacher looked out at all those graduates of yeshivas and parochial schools sitting in front of him and said, "You know where you are now?" And we responded "Yeah, we're at the Bronx High School of Science." If you are from New York or familiar with its culture, you must know that for a thirteen year old then, that was like being in heaven. It was the goal of our parent's lives for us to have been admitted there. But imagine our reaction when Dr. Something-or-Other looked out at the class and said, "Just so we understand each other, how many of you kids believe in that God junk?" Remember the Jewish concept that you can win or lose the World-to-Come in one moment? Let me tell you that there was only one kid in that class who won the World-to-Come. It wasn't me or any of the Catholic kids, it was one lone Jewish girl who had the courage to raise her hand.

As Jews increasingly seek to find spiritual values, they are going to find that kind of environment more uncomfortable. On the other hand, I think the culture itself may change and become more open to religious values, even in the public schools. I think it must change, just as America in general is becoming more spiritual and more concerned about finding itself religiously.

These are very difficult questions and as the American Jewish community changes, I think that their attitude about vouchers and funding may change. I know that I have been persuaded today, by listening to several of the earlier presentations, that the issue of funding for Jewish day schools is less important than the social justice issues that we are confronting as a community and as a people. There is a real need on the part of the American Jewish community for a serious reassessment. The goal of that reassessment must be the question "What is best for America?" That must be considered without any of the stereotypes that we have, without many of the church-state concerns that we have had over the years. We must only ask, "What's best for America?" Will vouchers make things better for the neediest part of America? Will they bring those children into contact with a better kind of education, one with the power to lift them up? I think that this is the essential question that an American Jew must ask, and that is the question that I am asking myself.

David Zweibel

I would like to build upon Barry Shrage's remarks, which are very important and fundamental. These are the proverbial best of times and also the worst of times. Those who are familiar with Jewish demographics in this country look with a sense of alarm at the extraordinarily high rate of intermarriage, wondering whether a generation or two from now our children and our grandchildren will really feel Jewish. Will they understand what that means and will they have a sense of belonging to the historical people that is the Jewish community?

The Talmud teaches the following parable, which I can't evaluate medically, but I know there is a lesson in it for us. It tells us: If someone is stung by a bee, the remedy is cold water. Don't use hot water because that is dangerous. If somebody is stung by a scorpion, the remedy is hot water, but don't use cold water because that is dangerous. The Talmudic sage continues to teach: But if someone is bitten by both a bee and a scorpion, he is in trouble. You can't use the cold water because while it may alleviate the problem of the bee, it is dangerous because of the scorpion bite. If you use hot water the reverse will be true.

This is an allegory for our circumstance as Jews in this imperfect world before the Messiah comes, before the redemption when we will live in that perfect society envisioned by Isaiah. This is a very imperfect time and we are beset by many different types of problems. Solutions that seem appropriate for certain contexts, may only create new sets of problems in other contexts. We have to find the appropriate balance between the hot water and the cold water.

It may well be that thirty or forty or fifty years ago, Jews saw themselves as a community of outsiders. They were a community of strangers who were not allowed to practice law in certain firms, who were not admitted into the country clubs or other settings for the larger American society and culture. To facilitate assimilation into the larger mainstream America, we developed policies regarding public school education that were phrased in terms of the question, "What's best for America?" Yet I suspect that when the Jewish community took its hard line stance on the separation of church and state, opposing all forms of assistance to religious education, it may have been intentionally to strengthen those agents of assimilation in our society, such as the public schools, which provided the flame for the melting pot.

That was an urgent priority for our community then. I submit that, given today's realities, the Jewish community has other, more urgent priorities. We've done such a marvelous job of assimilating, of melting into the larger society, that our real danger now is the danger of disappearing.

I believe the evidence is incontrovertible that Jewish education is the key to Jewish continuity and survival. If we don't recognize that as our number one priority, perhaps the time has come to take our fingers out of the hot water and put them into the cold water, and start reassessing what is best for us as a community.

This is my reading of the issues before us at this symposium. Just as there are arguments on both sides of the constitutional issues that have been raised, I think there are cogent arguments on both sides of these public policy questions. These are not simple issues and they do not yield simple solutions. But one thing that we, the Jewish community, have to include in our deliberations is an understanding of how these issues bear upon our most urgent priority, the strengthening of Jewish education.

Marvin Schick

Various reasons have been advanced for supporting vouchers—justice, the failure of the public school system, the notion of equality. On the other hand, the supporters of vouchers have been challenged by the potential problem of people in society whom we do not regard as our best citizens using the opportunity given to them by a voucher system to establish schools that do not advance the social good, but rather undermine it.

My response to both of these concerns is somewhat similar. One doesn't need to be a philosopher to recognize that every social arrangement, every contrivance established by the human species, is going to be filled with contradictions and difficulties, and with the necessity to make choices. When you add something to the balance on one side of the scale, you disadvantage something on the other side. Every kind of human relationship, whether it is marriage and the family or business relationships or personal friendships, all have the seeds of that problem of imbalance

Clearly there are contradictions inherent in vouchers as well. It is not simply a wonderful idea, where everything is triumphantly successful without any downside. That is not reality. But we have seen what fails, and now we have to opt for something else.

In respect to the second issue that was raised—the misuse of vouchers for antisocial education—I am sure that only a minuscule number of people would use vouchers to create something hurtful or wrong. Furthermore, whatever damage might arise in that way from a voucher system would be infinitesimally small compared to what we see happening in some segments of the public school system today.

What are the implications for the Jewish community? I would argue that if a voucher system were adopted which includes religious schools and which also passes constitutional muster, the implications for the Jewish community would still be minimal. It would not have a significant impact upon the day school movement. There is some small steady growth in the day school population. Most of that growth is within the Orthodox community, the Chassidic community, the yeshiva world. There is also an indication of growth in the Conservative, Reform and unaffiliated sectors, but proportionately that is rather small. You should be aware that there are fewer than 2000 students in all the non-Orthodox Jewish high schools in the United States, including Conservative, Reform and community sponsored schools. I don't think that number will change dramatically in the next decade. Maximally, it increases by fifty, seventy five or one hundred a year across the country. A voucher arrangement would not make much of a difference.

The reason is that we've already lost half of the Jews, Jews for whom Jewish schools are out of the question. It's not even a money question. For many, the cost of ten years of Jewish education, from nursery or kindergarten or Pre-K, does not equal the cost of a Bar or Bat Mitzvah. It is really a money issue for only a small minority and the assistance provided by vouchers would not become a significant factor in changing enrollment. Almost all Orthodox, including those who are marginal in the Orthodox world, send their children to a yeshiva or a day school. Clearly there will be no change in that trend. There will be more internal competition among schools in the community. New schools will challenge existing schools, and that competition might be healthy for the same reason that we've heard that competition will be healthy in the public school area.

If the American Jewish community abandons what I consider to be its reactionary position, a position which didn't make any sense when it was established decades ago and doesn't make any sense now, the roof isn't going to fall in—not on church-state separation, not on this republic, not anywhere else. Yet something else, something positive, may happen which I want you to consider and remember. Every so often on the subways of New York City I meet this vision of a teacher, or two or three teachers, taking a group of black children, first or second graders or maybe pre-schoolers, to a museum or a park. The children are usually holding hands, usually they walk in pairs, and the teacher has no trouble with these children. It is a beautiful sight to see children made in the image of God. You see the beauty of these children and you love them. But then just look at many of these same children five or six years later, and you could just cry. Look at what the system has done to them, the havoc which has been brought upon them, how they have been destroyed even in their youth. In God's name, at long last people have to realize that we've got to try something different. Let us feel the pain of these black families; let us share their needs. Let us see and sustain the beauty of these children. Let us care about children who are made in the image of God. That transcends anything else about vouchers.

David M. Pollack

Some years ago my wife and I began a discussion regarding schooling for our son. We have not stopped the discussion and we have not yet reached a decision. Our personal ambivalence, which reflects our quest for the best and most appropriate school, is one that is shared by parents all over the world, and the issue of vouchers is not a factor for us. I don't expect New York State to come up with vouchers very soon and I also don't expect the New York JCRC to come to a new position on vouchers very soon, despite the varying arguments that we heard here today reflecting both sides of the issue.

I want to share a few comments from the New York perspective. The first concerns how the public school system works for the Jewish community. In general, it has worked well. Barry Shrage gave us a wonderful personal example of how he finished eighth grade at a day school, then entered the Bronx High School of Science. Bronx Science and the three other academic high schools are disproportionately Jewish. It's a system that does happen to respond to and "cream off" people who are competitive. Over the past two weeks, however, there have been demonstrations at all of the academic high schools by a community-based, mostly black group asking why their children are not prepared to be competitive. That is a valid claim, an issue that we are not dealing with as a society.

Second, in December Governor Pataki signed a bill which begins dismantling the legacy of Ocean Hill-Brownsville and the restructuring of the New York school system. That was a failed Ford Foundation experiment. It was an attempt to give parents what turned out to be a false sense of empowerment and choice, under the guise of local control. But this experiment turned out to have a very significant effect upon the Jewish community. Approximately ten to fifteen per cent of Jews who were employed in New York City were employed either by the Board of Education or by contractors for the Board of Education. A very significant number of the employees of the school system were Jewish, and they started to be driven out. It became a significant Jewish issue, but as years go by it will grow exponentially less important because each early retirement offer from the Board of Education takes a disproportionate number of Jews.

Third, there is in New York City a pseudo-charter system called New Vision Schools. We now have schools that are run jointly by the Board of Education and community based organizations, including two run by East Brooklyn churches, one by South Bronx churches, one by the Abyssinian Baptist Church, one by the New York Mission Society and one from El Cuente. These are all value-laden schools and the Jewish community has not said one word about this phenomenon. No issues have been raised regarding these schools concerning church-state separation matters. They are providing education in a community supported, value-laden environment, but they are happening. There is also an all girls high school. The only parallel program that vaguely affects the Jewish community is a school which was put together by a number of Russian parents and professionals who wanted to have a school where they could teach music using Russian methods. They now have a small school run in conjunction with Goodman House.

In New York City about 45 percent of Jewish students are in public schools, 45 percent are in yeshivas and 10 percent are in non-parochial private schools. What this tells us is that we of the Jewish community have to figure out not only how to educate our students in yeshivas and day schools but how to meet the challenge of engaging Jewish students in varied environments or we will lose the battle for Jewish continuity.

Deborah Miller

It is almost impossible to think about public funding of my little Solomon Schechter Day School without, in some way, threatening the wall of separation of church and state. I would love to have more funds for our school. I would love to be able to accept more students, administer the school better, provide increased services, all of these things and more. Yet I think that it would be destructively self-serving if we were to go ahead and do that. My reason is clear. Our schools make a great effort to integrate the Jewish and general studies. To the extent that we do that and then try to fund this integration of general and Jewish studies with public funds, we are overstepping the bounds of separation. It is beyond me why the inhabitants of East Brunswick, New Jersey, should fund our teaching of Torah. I cannot think why the general populace would want to do that, particularly when the vast majority of Jews in East Brunswick are not interested themselves in doing that. If we are not prepared to tax ourselves, why should we even consider seeking or accepting the taxes of the general community?

A second issue has to do with the question of discrimination. At present we are free from any legal clauses of discrimination on the basis of religion because we are a religious institution. The minute we take public funds, do we still have the right to say, "No, you may not enroll in our school because you are not Jewish"? If we were to accept money that comes from general public taxation, would we have the right to turn children away on those grounds?

My third issue has to do with the basic purpose of our school, which is to provide Jewish education for Jewish children. Any outside public support—no matter how neutral it is—is an overstepping of bounds. Even something as neutral as the gift of a computer enables us to use our regular funds in another way, for instance, in giving our Jewish Studies teachers better training.

We are indeed rife with inconsistencies. We are already getting all kinds of funds from the state and federal governments. There is a textbook loan program. We have special services for the teaching of English as a second language, speech articulation, compensatory education and supplementary education. We have Eisenhower grants for teaching math and science. All of those thing are in place and we recognize their inconsistencies. Vouchers would be another giant step in the same direction. I think that as American Jews who have been the direct beneficiaries of the protection afforded by the wall of separation, we have to be very careful before we permit or pursue a fraying of the edges.

These remarks have been excerpted from the transcript of a lengthy and freewheeling discussion at the May 1997 conference.

Contributors

ELLIOT ABRAMS is President of the Ethics and Public Policy Center, Washington, D.C.

MICHAEL ARIENS is Professor of Law at St. Mary's University of San Antonio School of Law, San Antonio, TX.

JAY BERNSTEIN is co-chair of Advocates for Leadership in Educational Funding, Baltimore, MD.

MARSHALL J. BREGER is Professor of Law at the Columbus School of Law, Catholic University of America, Washington, D.C.

LARRY COHEN is co-chair of Advocates for Leadership in Educational Funding, Baltimore, MD.

JEREMY DAUBER is currently a Rhodes scholar at Oxford University, writing his doctoral dissertation on Hebrew and Yiddish literature.

ROBERT DESTRO is Professor of Law and Director of the Interdisciplinary Program in Law and Religion at the Columbus School of Law, Catholic University of America, Washington, D.C.

CHESTER E. FINN, JR. is the John M. Olin Fellow and co-chair of the Education Excellence Network at the Hudson Institute, Washington, D.C.

FLOYD FLAKE is a former member of the U. S. House of Representatives (D-6, NY) and pastor of the Allen African Methodist Episcopal Church, Jamaica, Queens, NY.

DAVID M. GORDIS is Director of The Susan and David Wilstein Institute of Jewish Policy Studies and President of Hebrew College, Brookline, MA.

JAY P. GREENE is Assistant Professor in the Department of Government, University of Texas at Austin.

MARCI A. HAMILTON is Professor of Law at the Benjamin N. Cardozo School of Law, Yeshiva University, New York, NY.

GEORGE HANUS is Chairman of the National Jewish Day School Scholarship Committee, Chicago, IL.

ZACHARY I. HELLER is Associate Director of The Susan and David Wilstein Institute of Jewish Policy Studies, Brookline, MA.

JEFFREY HENIG is Professor of Political Science and Director of the Center for Washington Area Studies at George Washington University, Washington, D.C.

SANFORD LEVINSON is Professor of Law and Government at the University of Texas, Austin, TX.

NATHAN LEWIN is a partner in the law firm of Miller, Cassidy, Larroca and Lewin, Washington, D.C.

AVRAM LYON is the Executive Director of the Jewish Labor Committee, New York, NY.

The Most Reverend JAMES T. MCHUGH is Bishop of Camden, New Jersey.

DEBORAH MILLER is the former Director of the Solomon Schechter Day School in East Brunswick, NJ.

MARTIN J. PLAX is Cleveland Area Director of the American Jewish Committee.

DAVID M. POLLACK is Associate Executive Director of the Jewish Community Relations Council of New York, NY.

RONALD D. ROTUNDA is Professor of Law at the University of Illinois College of Law, Champaign, IL.

JONATHAN SARNA is Professor in American Jewish History in the Department of Near Eastern and Judaic Studies at Brandeis University, Waltham, MA.

MARVIN SCHICK is President of the Rabbi Jacob Joseph School in Staten Island, NY and a consultant for the Avi Chai Foundation.

ALVIN I. SCHIFF is Professor of Education at the Azrieli Graduate School, Yeshiva University, New York, NY.

BARRY SHRAGE is President of the Combined Jewish Philanthropies of Boston, MA.

MELVIN SHRALOW is Co-chair of the Ad-hoc Committee on Vouchers of the Jewish Council on Public Affairs, and a partner in the law firm of White and Williams, Philadelphia, PA.

STEVEN R. SHAPIRO is Legal Director of the American Civil Liberties Union, New York, NY.

MARC D. STERN is Co-Director of the Commission on Law and Social Action of the American Jewish Congress.

JONATHAN S. TOBIN is Executive Editor of the Connecticut Jewish Ledger.

JOSEPH P. VITERITTI is Director of the Program on Education and Civil Society at the Robert F. Wagner Graduate School of Public Service, New York University.

EUGENE VOLOKH is Acting Professor of Law at the University of California, Los Angeles.

DAVID ZWEIBEL is Legal Counsel and Director of Government Affairs to Agudath Israel of America.